Article 13

The Right to Freedom of Expression

A Commentary on the United Nations Convention
on the Rights of the Child

Editors

André Alen, Johan Vande Lanotte, Eugeen Verhellen,
Fiona Ang, Eva Berghmans and Mieke Verheyde

Article 13

The Right to Freedom of Expression

By

Herdís Thorgeirsdóttir

Professor of Constitutional Law and Human Rights at the
Faculty of Law, Bifrost School of Business, Iceland

MARTINUS NIJHOFF PUBLISHERS
LEIDEN • BOSTON
2006

This book is printed on acid-free paper.

A Cataloging-in-Publication record for this book is available from the Library of Congress.

Cite as: H. Thorgeirsdóttir "Article 13. The Right to Freedom of Expression", in: A. Alen, J. Vande Lanotte, E. Verhellen, F. Ang, E. Berghmans and M. Verheyde (Eds.) *A Commentary on the United Nations Convention on the Rights of the Child* (Martinus Nijhoff Publishers, Leiden, 2006).

ISSN 1574-8626
ISBN-13: 978-90-04-14868-0
ISBN-10: 90-04-14868-X

Cover image by Nadia, 1 $^1/_2$ years old.

http://www.brill.nl

PRINTED IN THE NETHERLANDS

CONTENTS

LIST OF ABBREVIATIONS

ACHPR	African Charter on Human and Peoples' Rights 1981
ACHR	American Convention on Human Rights 1969
CCPR	International Covenant on Civil and Political Rights 1966
CERD	International Convention on the Elimination of all forms of Racial Discrimination 1966
CoE	Council of Europe
CRC	Convention on the Rights of the Child 1989
CRC Committee	UN Committee on the Rights of the Child
ECHR	European Convention on Human Rights and fundamental freedoms 1950
ECmHR	European Commission of Human Rights
ECtHR	European Court of Human Rights
EU	European Union
IACtHR	Inter-American Court of Human Rights
UDHR	Universal Declaration of Human Rights 1948
UN	United Nations
UNESCO	United Nations Educational, Scientific and Cultural Organisation
US	United States

AUTHOR BIOGRAPHY

Herdís Thorgeirsdóttir (Icelandic), Dr. Juris, Professor of Constitutional Law and Human Rights at the Faculty of Law of Bifrost School of Business in Iceland. She finished her doctoral degree at the Faculty of Law, University of Lund, Sweden. Her area of expertise is freedom of expression and the media from the perspective of comparative constitutional law and the European Convention on Human Rights. Her book Journalism Worthy of the Name: Freedom within the Press and the Affirmative Side of Article 10 under the European Convention on Human Rights, was published in May 2005 by Martinus Nijhoff Publishers. She has published articles on the topic in well-known and respected journals like the European Human Rights Law Review and Netherlands Quarterly of Human Rights. Dr. Thorgeirsdóttir works as an independent expert with the network of legal experts on the application of Community law on the equality between women and men for the European Commission. She is Vice-President of EWLA since March 2005 (European Women Lawyers' Association). She is a substitute member of the Venice Commission; the Council of Europe Commission for Democracy through Law since 2003. She has done pioneering work in gender equality matters in Iceland and was nominated for the gender equality prize for 2004 by the Equal Status Council for her initiatives in this area. She worked as a journalist and was editor and publisher of a popular monthly magazine for 8 years. She is the representative of the President of Iceland as chairperson of the Icelandic Literary Awards in 2004 and 2005. She studied journalism in London and has a BA degree in political science from the University of Iceland; an M.A.L.D. degree in international law from the Fletcher School of Law in Boston and a Doctor of Law degree in public international law from the Faculty of Law at the University of Lund in Sweden. She is the mother of four children (born 1987, 1993, 1994 and 1997).

TEXT OF ARTICLE 13

ARTICLE 13

1. The child shall have the right to freedom of expression; this right shall include freedom to seek, receive and impart information and ideas of all kinds, regardless of frontiers, either orally, in writing or in print, in the form of art, or through any other media of the child's choice.

2. The exercise of this right may be subject to certain restrictions, but these shall only be such as are provided by law and are necessary:

(a) For respect of the rights or reputations of others; or
(b) For the protection of national security or of public order (ordre public), or of public health or morals.

ARTICLE 13

1. L'enfant a droit à la liberté d'expression. Ce droit comprend la liberté de rechercher, de recevoir et de répandre des informations et des idées de toute espèce, sans considération de frontières, sous une forme orale, écrite, imprimée ou artistique, ou par tout autre moyen du choix de l'enfant.

2. L'exercice de ce droit ne peut faire l'objet que des seules restrictions qui sont prescrites par la loi et qui sont nécessaires:

(a) Au respect des droits ou de la réputation d'autrui; ou
(b) A la sauvegarde de la sécurité nationale, de l'ordre public, de la santé ou de la moralité publiques.

CHAPTER ONE

INTRODUCTION*

1. The present analysis aims to explore the meaning and significance of the freedom of expression as recognized in Article 13 of the United Nations Convention on the Rights of the Child.[1] It seeks to do so not only in relation to the CRC itself but also in the overall human rights context in light of jurisprudence and objectives. The entrenchment of children's rights in international law may conduce to a 'culture of child participation'[2] which may be gradually developing although overshadowed by louder and more powerful interests. An exciting challenge in exploring Article 13 of the CRC in this context is to add an additional dimension to our understanding of the nature of the freedom of expression. Aristotle said that man by nature is a political animal and the only animal whom nature has endowed with the gift of speech. Children with their own cluster of political rights have now been given the power of speech so they are no longer a mere voice indicating pleasure and pain but equipped with the means to have a more perfected impact on their lives and destinies than if simply regarded as a lower sort. Implied in the premises of this study is the changed vision of children as beings that must be taken seriously. Thinking about children as serious 'holders' of human rights is not intended to belittle their right to an innocent childhood or diminish the importance of providing them with the legal protection within the sphere of communication, which conditions their cognitive development. This is rather a question of rethinking about innocence and the role of children in contributing to our understanding of the world. Children may not have the same vocabulary as grown ups in expressing their opinions and ideas but the complex rhetoric of the worldly wise is not always speaking clearly. Hans Christian Andersen's famous fairy

---

* June 2005.
[1] Hereafter referred to as 'the CRC'.
[2] The term 'participation' does not only indicate presence or that one is a part of a group but also that one is actively involved and has some influence over decisions and actions as is the underlying premises of civil and political rights. The CRC Committee frequently encourages youth participation in societal matters *Cf.* CRC Committee, *Concluding Observations*: Cambodia (UN Doc. CRC/C/15/Add.128, 2000), paras. 33–34.

tale 'The Emperor's New Suit' had this core message: *Good heavens! Listen to the voice of an innocent child.*

2. Traditionally the right to freedom of expression has not been associated with children,[3] even though they enjoy freedom of expression under other international human rights treaties as well as regional ones. Despite the early 1924 Declaration on the Rights of the Child preceding the Universal Declaration of Human Rights, children are widely not 'factual' bearers of political rights.[4] The rights of millions of children are denied every day. Statistics show that in 2005 almost 448 million children are deprived of information, which they are entitled to under Articles 13 and 17 of the CRC. They lack access to television, radio, telephone or newspaper.[5] Without access to information children are deprived of the fundamental value of being informed about their environment, their society, their rights and opportunities. They are not able to participate effectively and have an impact on their lives and future. They are victims of a situation that excludes them and marginalizes and jeopardizes their future and chances for a better world. Independent of the definition of a child or the concept of childhood, children remain less equal than others although emphasis in the human rights rhetoric in recent years has been not only on the law protecting children but on recognizing that they are entitled to participate in decisions involving their own destinies. The CRC declares in its preamble that 'the child should be fully prepared to live an individual life in society, and be brought up in the spirit of the ideals proclaimed in the Charter of the United Nations, and in particular in the spirit of peace, dignity, tolerance, freedom, equality and solidarity.' In other words, children must be raised in consciousness that their energy and talents should also be devoted to the service of others, as stated in the 1959 UN Declaration of the Rights of the Child.

3. The CRC marked a decisive shift in the legal concept of the child within international law in its consistent application of a rights-based approach to children's issues. This is not least particularly relevant with regard to civil

---

[3] G. Van Bueren, *The International Law on the Rights of the Child* (The Hague, Martinus Nijhoff Publishers, 1998), p. 131. The author refers to the fact that neither of the two Declarations on the Rights of the Child include any reference to the child's freedom of expression; and that in the original draft for the CRC submitted by Poland, the child's right to freedom of expression was not mentioned.

[4] *Cf.* CRC Committee, *General Comment No 2 (2002) The role of independent national human rights institutions in the promotion and protection of the rights of the child* (UN Doc. CRC/GC/2002/2, 2002), para. 5.

[5] C. Bellamy, *Childhood under Threat. Official summary of The state of the World's Children in 2005* (New York/Geneva, UNICEF, December 2004), p. 19.

and political rights. The adoption of the CRC in 1989 reflected the international consensus on a new vision of children – no longer as mere objects of protection who have 'needs', but as human beings who enjoy 'rights'.[6] The Human Rights Committee has observed that 'as individuals, children benefit from all of the civil rights enunciated in' the CCPR.[7] Consistent with this view, the State may not accord less respect to the right of children and adolescents to freedom of expression. The CRC reinforces this conclusion by guaranteeing the right of youth to freedom of expression in terms that are identical to those of Article 19 of the CCPR.

4. Freedom of expression is a cornerstone of democratic rights and freedoms, a basic civil and political right, accordingly laid down in all respective human rights instruments (*Cf. infra* Chapter 2). In its very first session in 1946, before any human rights declarations or treaties had been adopted, the UN General Assembly adopted resolution 59(I) stating '*Freedom of information is a fundamental human right and [. . .] the touchstone of all the freedoms to which the United Nations is consecrated.*' The resolution is a clear indicator of the instrumental nature of this right. It is important as an instrumental freedom for the progress and continuity of a democratic society. The further realisation of human rights is unthinkable without people exercising their freedom of expression. Freedom of expression is a prerequisite for basic democratic governance as free elections are to ensure the free expression of the opinion of the people in the choice of their legislature. Citizens cannot exercise their right to vote effectively or take part in public decision-making if they do not have free access to information and ideas and are not able to express and form their views freely. Freedom of expression is commonly associated with communicative rights. (*Cf. infra* Nos. 35–40).

5. Freedom of expression is also subjectively valuable to each individual for his/her personal growth and cognitive development. It is as essential for self-knowledge as air and light for physical existence.

6. Apart from the instrumental value freedom of expression has an intrinsic value because it is important in itself,[8] and not only reducible to its utility to the interests of society or oneself.

---

[6] *Cf.* Mary Robinson in a statement to the United General Assembly Special Session on Children on 9th May 2002. The text of Mrs. Robinson's address was accessed on the website of the United Nations High Commissioner for Human Rights: <http://www.unhchr.ch/>

[7] Human Rights Committee, *General Comment No. 17: Rights of the child (Art. 24)* (U.N. Doc. HRI/GEN/1/Rev.1, 1994), p. 23, para. 2.

[8] *Cf.* R. Dworkin, *Life's Dominion: An Argument about Abortion, Euthanasia and Individual Freedom* (New York, Vintage Books, 1993), pp. 69–74.

7. Article 13 of the CRC falls in the category of civil rights and when interpreted together with surrounding articles it provides the argument for the child's right to participate 'so that it can fully assume its responsibilities within the community' as stated in the Preamble to the CRC. This category of rights in the CRC serves the same purpose as parallel categories in other human rights instruments falling under the rubric of civil and political rights. These are not only substantive rights but also procedural rights. The classical rationale behind freedom of expression is that it enhances not only participation of individuals in society and hence serves the purpose of democratic ideals but furthermore is a necessary prerequisite for the self-development of each and every individual. Affording children this right in a special instrument in addition to the other instruments that do not distinguish between children and adults in being holders of this right, is a recognition of the significance of children acquiring cognitive, emotional, social, moral competencies absorbing influence from the environment and expressing their reactions, opinions and sentiments. As stated in the 1924 Declaration of Geneva: 'The child must be given the means needed for its normal development, both materially and spiritually'. The CRC makes clear that parental direction and guidance to children must be provided in accordance with the child's evolving capacities. It is through participation that children are empowered to take greater responsibility for the exercise of their own rights as they gain confidence and competence to make informed choices.[9]

8. The method of analysis in this study involves a brief comparison between Article 13 of the CRC with related regional and international human rights provisions protecting freedom of expression and description of the main similarities and differences between the protection offered by Article 13 of the CRC and these other instruments basically by focusing on the wording of the text. Special emphasis is given to the fact that the child's right to freedom of opinion is not protected explicitly under Article 13.

9. The juridical international scope of Article 13 of the CRC is examined in depth in Chapter 3 of this survey through a critical analysis of the text of the CRC. The content of the right as well as the scope and nature of the corresponding State obligations are looked into. The analysis is assisted by recourse to the 'Travaux Preparatoires' of the Convention,[10] and of parallel

---

[9] *Cf.* G. Lansdown, 'Promoting Children's Participation in Democratic Decision-Making' (*Unicef, Innocenti Insight*, February 2001), p. 6.

[10] Article 49 of the Vienna Convention on the Law of Treaties (adopted on 23 May 1969, entered into force 27 January 1980) permits this preparatory work to be used to aid interpretation of a treaty where its provisions are unclear.

human rights instruments. The concluding observations issued by the Committee on the Rights of the Child[11] in response to States Parties reports and its discussions with States in relation to those reports, its general comments, and its recommendations at the end of a general discussion day, are also essential to describe the substantive nature of this right also with reference to the comparative practice and jurisprudence of other UN treaty bodies and the comparative jurisprudence of regional organs for the protection of human rights. The European Convention on Human Rights jurisprudence is of particular interest because of its effective control machinery and wealth of case law, which has increased human rights awareness not only on a pan-European dimension and within the European Union but also around the world. This should provide an authoritative illustration of the substantial protection of Article 13 of the CRC aided by contextual analysis of this provision read in light of the CRC as a whole and also from a dynamic perspective in the light of comprehensive academic literature.

---

[11] Hereafter referred to as 'the CRC Committee'.

CHAPTER TWO

COMPARISON WITH RELATED HUMAN RIGHTS PROVISIONS

1. Freedom of Expression in Public International Law

10. Freedom of expression is guaranteed in international law as well as regional human rights treaties and it is widely guaranteed in many of the world's constitutions. Children are beneficiaries of the freedom of expression rights in these treaties just like adults. Moreover, there are special provisions in these and other treaties relating to children in particular, either implicitly or explicitly. Article 19 of the UDHR,[12] adopted in 1948 submits:

> 'Everyone has the right to freedom of opinion and expression; this right includes freedom to hold opinions without interference and to seek, receive and impart information and ideas through any media and regardless of frontiers.'

11. The difference between Article 13 of the CRC and parallel provisions in other instruments can best be described by the formal and literal structure of the relevant guarantees. The structure of Article 13 of the CRC is similar to all the other related regional and international freedom of expression provisions in that it grants the right in the first paragraph(s) and significantly circumscribes it in the latter. Article 13 is like the other provisions not absolute. Article 13(2)(a) makes reference to the strength of potentially competing interests – to the possibility of the right to be outweighed or overridden and Article 13(2)(b) describes circumstances in which the exercise of the child's right to freedom of expression may nevertheless be restricted.

12. Article 19 of the UDHR which is not a binding legal instrument provides the model for parallel provisions in other human rights treaties. There is an affinity between the International Covenant of Civil and Political Rights, which was adopted in 1966 while its Article 19 was formulated at a very early stage of the elaboration of the CCPR. Drawing on and developing the Article 19 of the UDHR, the CCPR provision has several noteworthy elements which are of interest for further analysis of the freedom of expression as

---

[12] Universal Declaration of Human Rights, G.A. Res. 217 A (III), Annex, adopted on 10 December 1948.

protected in various instruments. Freedom of opinion is protected separately in Article 19(1) and distinguished from freedom of thought in Article
18. The right to hold opinions is 'without interference', excluding any restriction whatever and hence appears to be absolute.[13] Article 19(3), on the other
hand, allows expressly for limitation upon the freedom of expression. This
distinction is of extreme significance with regard to analysis of the extent
of protection afforded to the political right of forming an opinion as opposed
to the right to express an opinion. (*Cf. infra* Nos. 20–23).

13. Article 10 of the ECHR, adopted in 1950, is the oldest binding human
rights provision of the ones included here, protecting freedom of expression and to a large extent modelled after Article 19 of the UDHR. The structure of Article 10 is like that of the other provisions in the category of civil
and political rights in the ECHR, ranging from privacy (Article 8), thought,
conscience (Article 9) to opinion, expression (Article 10) and association
(Article 11). Under Article 10(1) freedom of expression includes freedom to
hold opinions and to receive and impart information and ideas without
interference by public authority and regardless of frontiers. The second
paragraph identifies the criteria upon which an interference with the rights
may be justified. Unlike Article 19 of the CCPR, the freedom of expression
clause in the ECHR does not explicitly mention the form of expression protected, *e.g.* orally, in writing, in print, in the form of art or through any
other media of his choice as does the younger instrument. Nor does it protect the expression of 'all kinds' of information and ideas. Protection of the
specific means by which the opinion is expressed is elaborated in the ECHR
jurisprudence but from the text of the article it is not completely clear.

14. Freedom of opinion on the other hand is not exempted from the restriction clause in Article 10(2) of the ECHR, which illustrates that the freedom
of opinion is not unsusceptible to external forces with regard to protection
as the *forum internum*. As a case in point, the French version of Article 19
of the CCPR '*Nul ne peut être inquiéte pour ses opinions*' is quite different in
substance and style to the English version of Article 19[14] as well as the wording in Article 10 of the Convention.

---

[13] *Cf.* K. J. Partsch, 'Freedom of Conscience and Expression, Political Freedoms' in: L. Henkin
(ed.), *The International Bill of Right* (New York, Columbia University Press, 1981), p. 218.
[14] Annotations on the Text of the Draft International Covenants on Human Rights (prepared by the Secretary-General), 10 U.N. GAOR, Annexes (Agenda Item No. 28) 50, UN Doc.
A/2929, Ch. VI, (Official Records of the General Assembly, Tenth Session 1955), para. 121.

15. The American Convention on Human Rights (1969) does not make this distinction between thought and opinion and omits the latter completely, protecting conscience and religion under Article 12 and freedom of thought and expression in Article 13(1). Both thought and expression are subject to subsequent imposition of liability, which shall be expressly established by law to ensure respect for the rights or reputations of others (Article 13(2)(a)) and the protection of national security, public order, or public health or morals (Article 13(2)(b)). It is expressly stated in Article 13(3) that the right of expression may not 'be restricted by indirect methods or means, such as the abuse of government or private controls over newsprint, radio broadcasting frequencies, or equipment used in the dissemination of information, or by any other means tending to impede the communication and circulation of ideas and opinions.' Evidently this provision not only prohibits obstacles in the way of communication but also abuse of media and other means to restrict expression which may imply prohibition of indoctrination of the mind.[15]

16. The African Charter of Human and Peoples' Rights, adopted in 1981 protects freedom of conscience and 'free practice of religion' in Article 8 and the right of every individual to receive information in Article 9(1) and subsequently in Article 9(2) to express and disseminate his opinions within the law.

17. Article 11 of the EU Charter of Fundamental Rights is modelled after Article 10(1) of the ECHR in submitting in its Article 11(1) that freedom of expression includes 'the right to hold opinions, and to receive and impart information and ideas without interference by public authority and regardless of frontiers.' It omits the word seek and also the last sentence of the ECHR Article 10(1) allowing States to require the licensing of broadcasting.

18. *Prima facie*, Article 19 of the CCPR seems to offer the broadest guarantee for freedom of expression and opinion. Freedom of opinion is guaranteed on the horizontal level as well as from public interference. This leads to speculation of the extent of protection given to the forum internum in the other instruments as will be discussed at further length in chapter 3 on freedom of opinion. For the time being it is sufficient to say that freedom of opinion enjoys prima facie more protection in Article 19(1) of the CCPR than in Article 10(1) of the ECHR – at least on the surface.

---

[15] *Cf.* IACtHR, Advisory Opinion OC-5/85 of November 13, 1985, Series A, No. 5.

19. The right to seek information is not explicitly protected under Article 10 of neither the ECHR nor the African Charter while it is protected under the CCPR as well as the ACHR. None of the instruments – including Article 13 of the CRC, which is modelled after Article 19 CCPR[16] – protects opinion separately as in Article 19(1) of the CCPR. Article 13 of the CRC does not mention opinion. The preceding Article 12(1) of the CRC submits that 'States parties shall assure to the child who is capable of forming his or her owns views the right to express those views freely in all matters affecting the child, the views of the child being given due weight in accordance with the age and maturity of the child'. While the right to be heard is a key factor of Article 12 of the CRC it would evidently amount to little if the child was not also guaranteed the right to form his/her views as is the objective of the rights to seek, receive and impart information and ideas of all kinds, enshrined in Article 13 of the CRC. It may be stated that 'views without information are as worthless as a speech without an audience'.[17]

2. Excluding Freedom of Opinion from Article 13(1) of the CRC

20. The drafting history of both the CCPR and prior to that the ECHR and even later the CRC indicates that unlike ideological premises lead to different meanings attached to this freedom. The separation of the concept of opinion from expression had been a topic of much speculation during the drafting stages of Article 19 of the CCPR in the 1950s and early 1960s and also within the Human Rights Committee just a few years before the drafting of the parallel provision of the CRC. The Chairman of the Human Rights Committee had questioned the significance of protecting opinion separately in Article 19(1), i.e. whether protecting opinion absolutely meant very little, during discussions of draft General Comment on Article 19. 'Holding an opinion could not be interfered with if no one knew about it. Some phrase should perhaps be added to make clear what was being protected. Perhaps it was the right freely to form opinions without their being imposed, either directly or indirectly, publicly or in private'.[18]

---

[16] S. Detrick, *A Commentary on the United Nations Convention on the Rights of the Child* (Hague/Boston/London, Martinus Nijhoff Publishers, 1999), p. 233.

[17] K. Boyle, 'Article 19, The International Centre Against Censorship' in: A. Eide and S. Skogly (eds.), *Human Rights and the Media*, 1986, Norwegian Institute of Human Rights Publications, p. 107.

[18] D. McGoldrick, *The Human Rights Committee: Its Role in the Development of the International Covenant on Civil and Political Rights* (Oxford, Clarendon Press, 1991), p. 460. Human Rights Committee, *General Comment No. 10: Freedom of expression* (Art. 19) (UN Doc. CCPR/C/21/Add.2, 1983).

21. The preparatory work of the CCPR supports the view that freedom of opinion and freedom of expression are separate freedoms, with separate characters. Freedom of opinion, according to the drafters, was a purely private matter, belonging to the realm of the mind, while the latter was a public matter, or a matter of human relationship, which should be subject to legal as well as moral restraint. It was recognized that a person was invariably conditioned or influenced by the external world, it was generally agreed that no law could regulate his opinion and *no power* could dictate what opinion he should not entertain. The decision was made, therefore, to treat the right to freedom of opinion separately.[19]

22. Originally, the English version of Article 19(1) CCPR read: 'Everyone shall have the right to freedom of opinion without interference'. This sentence was later changed to read: 'Everyone shall have the right to hold opinions without interference.'[20] There is a noticeable difference between the two phrases where the latter may be seen as protecting less, *e.g.* merely the right to *hold* an opinion, whereas the original sentence, which was abandoned in the end-result, may be interpreted as offering protection to the process of *forming* an opinion. The change of wording, during the drafting stages, from the 'right to freedom of opinion' to 'the right to hold opinions' is a token of the broader meaning of 'the right to freedom of opinion' entailing the right to form an opinion with the correlative duty imposed on the opinion-makers. As originally proposed, the phrase 'without interference' was followed by the phrase 'by governmental action'. There were two views regarding this point. One was that Article 19(1) was intended to protect the individual only against government interference. The other view was that Article 19(1) should protect the individual against all kinds of interference.[21] It was discussed that private financial interests and monopoly control of media information could be as harmful as government interference, and that the latter should not be singled out to the exclusion of the former.[22] Hence it may be asserted that freedom of opinion is protected from private as well as public interference. It is, however, still disputed whether the right to freedom of opinion in Article 19(1) is the right to form an opinion, which

---

[19] Annotations on the Text of the Draft International Covenants on Human Rights (prepared by the Secretary-General), 10 UN GAOR, Annexes (Agenda Item No. 28) 50, UN Doc. A/2929, Chapter VI, paras. 119–138 (Official Records of the General Assembly, Tenth Session, 1955).

[20] *Ibid.*, para. 121.

[21] *Ibid.*, Chapter VI, para. 122.

[22] U.N. GAOR Third Committee, 16th Session, 1961, U.N. Doc. A/5000, paras. 5–35 (Official Records of the General Assembly, Sixteenth Session, 5 December 1961), para. 24.

would subsequently entail protection from being manipulated by unilateral political propaganda or being 'brainwashed'.[23] It is in any case extremely difficult to draw the line of permissible and impermissible interference with freedom of opinion under Article 19(1).[24] Interference with expressed opinions is tangible while for example the delicate process of reaching a conclusion in a political controversy may be apt to insidious constraints or manipulative tactics in the media or by other forces. 'Partsch has questioned whether the complex problem of protecting a person's opinion against interference by others can be solved in this global and absolute manner.[25]

23. The fact that opinion is not protected separately in Article 10 of the ECHR as in Article 19 of the CCPR has provided rationale to those who want to reduce the right to opinion to merely the right to hold one and not to form one; something equivalent to freedom of thought. That argument seems lame in light of the fact that the distinct aspects of thought, belief and opinion are widely protected in separate provisions, as is the case in CCPR and the ECHR. The Canadian Charter of Rights and Freedoms enlists as fundamental freedoms ascribed to everyone the freedom of thought, belief, opinion and expression.

24. The question of whether there is a distinction between 'thought' and 'opinion' has been raised, both in relation to Article 19 of the CCPR and Article 10 of the ECHR. Some maintain that the concepts, though not identical are close to each other in meaning; others believe that the two concepts are complementary and some say that in both Articles the right to hold an opinion is really a truism and therefore superfluous.[26] If, like mentioned during the drafting stages of the CCPR, holding an opinion is a superfluous truism, why then bother to protect it, from whom or what? It is tempting to draw the conclusion from the drafting process that the original intention was to protect the formulation stage but adding the verb to 'hold' in the final draft is a sign of tentativeness. 'There is an interplay and similarity between the freedoms of thought and opinion. The concepts are

---

[23] D. McGoldrick, *The Human Rights Committee: Its Role in the Development of the International Covenant on Civil and Political Rights*, *o.c.* (note 18), p. 460.

[24] *Cf.* M. Nowak, *U.N. Covenant on Civil and Political Rights: CCPR Commentary* (Kehl/Strasbourg/Arlington, N.P. Engel, 1993), p. 340.

[25] K.J. Partsch, 'Freedom of Conscience and Expression, Political Freedoms', *l.c.* (note 13), pp. 217–18.

[26] U.N. Doc. A/2929, chapter VI, para. 123.*Cf.* H. Thorgeirsdóttir, *Journalism Worthy of the Name: Freedom within the Press and the Affirmative Side of Article 10 of the European Convention on Human Rights* (Leiden/Boston, Martinus Nijhoff Publishers, 2005), pp. 157–160.

certainly complementary to each other but definitely of different characters. Thought is an internal phenomenon referring to a process. Opinion is
the result of a thought process or of receiving information and ideas from,
as relevant, the media. Thoughts can be of all kinds, not necessarily formulated like an opinion, which brings thought closer to a conviction.[27] It is
ill-founded not to make a distinction between thought and opinion, even if
both are part of the realm of the mind and both essential to the liberty of
the mind. Thought can be random where opinion is usually decisive. Thought
is open-ended and opinion conclusive. Thought may be said to character-
ize the first step, opinion the second and so forth. Opinion is in essence a
consistent advancement of thought. Opinion, need not however, be a logi-
cal evolution of a thinking process. It can be a reverberation from the environment. Just like one starts humming a hit song, one's mind can function
as an echo chamber for something often heard and seen. The forming of
opinion is not a final stage but subject to changes and alterations. Media
coverage may induce hasty changes in public opinion. Opinion is not necessarily as strong a term as conviction but decisive all the same when it
comes to making a political choice.[28]

25. It is a limited interpretation of this freedom to maintain that it is simply referring to the content of expression in a narrow sense as the subject
matter of expression. The intention with the protection of this right was
not superfluous. The bounds of protection given in respect of the forum
internum is, however, not determined with regard to opinion while the
freedom of thought and conscience under Article 9 of the ECHR are absolute.
Freedom of opinion under Article 10 is not an unqualified right and cannot
hence be a redundancy.

26. The ECtHR has reiterated that requiring proof of the truth of value judgments is impossible to fulfil and that such a requirement would infringe
freedom of opinion itself, which is a fundamental part of the right secured
by Article 10 of the ECHR,[29] albeit value judgments without any factual basis
may be excessive and hence subject to restrictions. This submission goes
to show that the Court clearly distinguishes between opinions as value judgments and freedom of thought, which is absolute.

---

[27] K. J. Partsch, 'Freedom of Conscience and Expression, Political Freedoms', l.c. (note 13),
p. 217.
[28] H. Thorgeirsdóttir, o.c. (note 26), pp. 153–155.
[29] ECtHR, *Lingens* v. *Austria*, Judgment of 8 July 1986, *Publications of the Court*, Series A, 103,
para. 46.

27. It is quite clear from the case-law that the freedoms in Article 10 of the ECHR entail the right to form an opinion in a free manner, *e.g.* without unnatural external pressures and misleading practices. The fact that freedom of opinion in Article 10 is subject to restrictions in the same manner as uttered expressions *may render* the right even more meaningful. Forming an opinion is a delicate process, where manipulative techniques are in breach of the Convention.[30] The emphasis in the Court's case-law on this right as one of the basic conditions for each individual's self-fulfilment suggests that opinion-formation must be taken into account, being a part of individual maturity.[31]

28. Freedom of opinion, which is protected separately and absolutely in Article 19(1) of the CCPR is omitted from Article 13(1), which is modelled after the former. The impending analysis will hence focus on the relevance of this textual omission to the child's enjoyment of this right. (*Cf. infra* No. 41).

---

[30] *Cf.*, H. Thorgeirsdóttir, *o.c.* (note 26), p. 164.
[31] ECtHR, Nos. 11553/85 and 11658/85 joined, *Hodgson and Others* v. *United Kingdom*, Decision of 9 March 1987, D.R .51, p. 143.

CHAPTER THREE

SCOPE OF ARTICLE 13

1. *Introduction: Background and Context*

1.1 *Reservations and Reluctance*

29. The international standards provided for in the CRC – while widely not binding without legislative implementation – are all the same relevant sources for interpreting rights domestically.[32] The United States and Somalia are the only countries in the world that have not ratified the Convention, although ratification would not give the CRC the force of law in the US or any coercive effect in domestic law. A prevailing view within the US is that freedom of expression is adequately protected by the First Amendment to the US Constitution. It may however be questioned with regard to the protection of freedom of expression in the CRC whether the holistic approach to children's rights in general contradicts the view of freedom of speech as being a negative liberty rather than as a positive claim right as the civil and political rights in the CRC may be interpreted in light of the Convention as a whole, imposing indirect duties and liabilities upon private media corporations as well as authorities.[33] Traditionally the US has recognized civil and political rights – and its representatives were enthusiastic about this particular category of rights during the preparation of the CRC. Economic, social and cultural rights such as the right to education,[34] health care and adequate standard of living are not recognized rather than as the political results of freedom of speech and other negative liberties that may pave the way for positive goods. This view contends that as long as individuals have the rights to life, liberty, and property, they will always have the freedom

---

[32] *Cf.* R. v. Sharpe [2001] 1 S.C.R. 45. Internet: http://www.lexum.umontreal.ca/doc/csc-scc/en/index/html; 194 Dominion Law Reports (4th) 1; 146 British Columbia Appeal Cases 161; 150 Canadian Criminal Cases (3d) 321; 39 Criminal Reports (5th) 72; [2001] S.C.J. no. 3 (Quicklaw).

[33] *Cf.* CRC Committee, *Recommendation: The Private Sector as Service Provider and its Role in Implementing Child Rights* (UN Doc. CRC/C/121, 2002).

[34] Education in the US occurs under a highly decentralized system with funding and curriculum decisions taking place mostly at the local level and educational standards are generally set by State agencies not the Federal Government.

to obtain the means to exercise their freedom of speech.[35] The US has not ratified the International Covenant on Economic, Social and Cultural Rights[36] where Article 13 prescribes, *inter alia*, that primary educa-tion shall be compulsory and available free to all.

30. Many States Parties to the CRC made general reservations concerning provisions considered incompatible with Islamic law,[37] referring in rather general terms to national legislation taking account of the interest of the child and the need to safeguard its physical and mental integrity,[38] as provided for in provisions of the Penal Code, in particular those sections relating to breaches of public order, to public decency and to the incitement of minors to immorality and debauchery. Algeria referred to a provision in the information code which banned any foreign publication with illustrations, narratives, information or insertion contrary to 'Islamic morality, national values or human rights or advocate racism, fanaticism and treason. Further, such publications must contain no publicity or advertising that may promote violence and delinquency'. Some CoE Member States declared that Article 13 of the CRC would be applied provided that it would not affect legal restrictions in accordance with Article 10 of the ECHR.[39] There were also reservations with regard to the right of the child to the participatory freedoms in Articles 12–16 that they should be exercised with respect for parental authority.

31. While the CRC widely does not form part of domestic law, it provides an international standard, and the work of the CRC Committee may contribute to what become supranational paradigms by shedding light on ideological and technical controversies; for example with regard to definitions of what constitutes harmful speech; how children are not to be discriminated against in accessing information and what are essential State obligations in ensuring these rights to children. These dilemmas are ultimately fostered by the culture of the States Parties to the treaty although the ratification of the CRC may mean little more than a gesture to pay tribute to growing consensus about fundamental rights. On the other hand, such consensus is also facilitated with growing interest in children's rights with

---

[35] *Cf. supra* No 2 concerning children's lack of information.
[36] CESCR opened for signature in 1966 and entered into force in 1976.
[37] Concerning provisions incompatible with Islamic Law. *Cf.* Afghanistan upon signature 27 September 1990.
[38] *Cf.* The reservation of Algeria, 26 January 1990.
[39] *Cf.* The reservation of Austria, 26 August 1990.

their own enhanced participation. Although the CRC guarantees to children the right to seek information, a child cannot resort to Article 13 of the CRC in claiming that his/her right in seeking information is violated under the CRC, as it does not incorporate a petitioning system to remedy breaches of the Convention.[40]

1.2   A Contextual Approach

32. The CRC Committee's Guidelines for Initial Reports require that States Parties provide relevant information, including the principal legislative, judicial, administrative or other measures in force; factors and difficulties encountered and progress achieved in implementing the relevant provisions of the Convention; and implementation priorities and specific goals for the future in respect of freedom of expression in Article 13.[41] The process of the subsequent periodic reporting is considered to be an integral part of the actual implementation of the CRC.[42] This method has also received extensive, and frequently scathing, criticism[43] although also recognized that the writing of reports provides an opportunity to assess the condition and status of children, and to plan measures for reform.[44]

33. In the CRC Committee's Guidelines for Periodic Reports, the provisions of the Convention have been grouped in clusters with a view to assisting States Parties in the preparation of their reports. This approach reflects the Convention's holistic perspective of children's rights: that they are indivisible and interrelated, and that equal importance should be attached to each and every right recognized therein. States are requested to describe the measures that, for instance, the media have taken to promote understanding of the principles and provisions of the Convention by the mass

---

[40] *Cf.* G. Van Bueren, *o.c.* (note 3), p. 132.

[41] CRC Committee, *General guidelines regarding the form and content of initial reports to be submitted by States Parties under Article 44, paragraph 1(a), of the Convention* (UN Docs. CRC/C/5, 1991 and CRC/C/7, 1991, Annex III).

[42] On the reporting procedure before the CRC Committee, see in general M. Verheyde and G. Goedertier, 'Articles 43–45: The Committee on the Rights of the Child', in: A. Alen, J. Vande Lanotte, F. Verhellen, F. Ang, E. Berghmans and M. Verheyde (eds.), *A Commentary on the United Nations Convention on the Rights of the Child* (Leiden/Boston, Martinus Nijhoff Publishers, 2005), 50p; and on the reporting guidelines more specifically, *Ibid.*, No. 19–25.

[43] J. Connors, 'An Analysis and Evaluation of the System of State Reporting' in: A. F. Bayefsky (ed.), *The UN Human Rights Treaty System in the 21st Century* (The Hague, Kluwer Law International, 2000), p. 4.

[44] J. Karp, 'Reporting and the Committee on the Rights of the Child' in: in A. F. Bayefsky (ed.), *The UN Human Rights Treaty System in the 21st Century* (The Hague, Kluwer Law International, 2000), p. 35.

media and by information and publishing agencies.[45] The CRC's uniqueness stems from the fact that it is the first legally binding international instrument to incorporate the full range of human rights (children's civil and political rights as well as their economic, social and cultural rights), thus giving all rights equal emphasis. The holistic approach to the CRC is apparent in the request to States with reporting on measures to combat discrimination; for instance measures that have been taken to prevent and eliminate attitudes to and prejudice against children contributing to social or ethnic tension, racism and xenophobia.[46] There is a link between Article 2 of the CRC submitting that the States Parties shall respect and ensure the rights set forth in the Convention to each child within their jurisdiction without discrimination of any kind and Article 13(2).

34. Article 13 of the CRC must be read in context of the Convention as a whole. The right to freedom of expression is closely related to the child's right to express views and have them taken seriously under Article 12. There is also a relationship between Article 13 and Article 14 on freedom of thought, conscience and religion and on freedom of association in Article 15. Article 16 is also of relevance to the interpretation of the child's right to freedom of expression stating that no child 'shall be subjected to arbitrary or unlawful interference with his or her home or correspondence, or to unlawful attacks on his or her honour or reputation.' Article 17 stipulates that States Parties recognize the important function of the mass media and that the child has access to information and material of legitimate interest. Article 27 stating that States Parties must recognize the right of every child to a standard of living adequate to physical, mental, spiritual, moral and social development and Article 28 submitting the child's right to education are also important in relation to Article 13 (*Cf. infra No.* 72). In view of the principles contained in Article 29(1)(d) of the Convention, which stipulates that the education of the child shall be directed to 'the preparation of the child for responsible life in a free society, in the spirit of understanding, peace, tolerance, equality of sexes, and friendship among all peoples, ethnic, national, religious groups and persons of indigenous origin', the teaching

---

[45] *Cf.* CRC Committee, *Day of General Discussion on the Child and the Media* (UN Doc. CRC/C/50, Annex IC, 1996), para. 22; *Cf.* CRC Committee, *Day of General Discussion on Implementing child rights in early childhood* (UN Doc. CRC/C/137, 2004), paras. 8–9, and (UN Doc. CRC/C/143, 2005), paras. 532–563.

[46] *Cf.* CRC Committee, *Concluding Observations: Luxembourg* (UN Doc. CRC/C/15/Add. 250, 2005), paras. 18–21.

of values is an important dimension that should be incorporated in the curricula at all levels of schooling. School curricula materials should be revised accordingly.[47]

1.3   The Instrumental Value

35. Freedom of expression, if properly protected, will enable the child to develop its mind and its self in society with others and grow into a citizen participating in public life as such and not merely as a mindless consumer. The instrumental value of freedom of expression includes the role in generating social and political incentives. It is hence of interest to question whether the right guaranteed in Art. 13 CRC may be interpreted as having greater weight and scope, *e.g.* not only to foster societal responsibility in the child by communicating compassion[48] but also whether it can be taken as an indicator that children should have a greater active role in shaping the environment that either makes them or breaks them. In other words, this is a question of whether children are 'fit for democracy?' Although it was not the intention of the drafters of the CRC to grant children voting rights it may be reasoned that the claim for direct political participation in the form of franchise for all may be derived from this right? As pointed out by the representative of Portugal in 1988, the child must be 'considered from a dual perspective: as an object of protection and as a possessor of rights'.[49] The title of the instrument confirms that the child is no less a possessor of rights as a suggestion of the title 'A draft convention on the protection of the child' was rejected.[50]

36. In one of its oldest freedom of expression cases, the European Court of Human Rights observed, '[f]reedom of expression constitutes one of the essential foundations of a democratic society and one of the basic conditions for its progress and for each individual's self fulfilment'.[51]

---

[47] CRC Committee, *Concluding Observations: Lebanon* (UN Doc. CRC/C/15/Add.54, 1996), para. 33.
[48] *Cf.* Wording of CRC Preamble, referred to *supra* No. 2.
[49] Travaux Préparatoires (UN Doc. E/CN.4/1989/48, 1989), pp. 5–8, 139–143. *Cf.* also S. Detrick, *o.c.* (note 16), p. 625.
[50] *Travaux Préparatoires* (UN Doc. E/CN.4/1989/48, 1989), pp. 5–8; in S. Detrick, *o.c.* (note 16), pp. 139–143.
[51] ECtHR, *Handyside* v. *the United Kingdom,* Judgment of 7 December 1976, *Publications of the Court*, Series A, 24, para. 49.

37. Realizing the political nature of freedom of expression to its fullest is blocked by the threshold of not being able to express one's will in the choice of the legislature.[52]

38. The CRC Committee has encouraged States to respect the rights of children less than 18 years to participate in political activities.[53] In the light of Articles 12 to 17 of the CRC, the Committee has recommended that a State Party amend its legislation, guidelines issued by the Ministry of Education and school regulations to facilitate children's active participation in decision-making processes and in political activities both within and outside schools and ensure that all children fully enjoy their right to freedom of association and expression.[54]

39. The CRC Committee submitted in a general comment that while adults and children alike need independent institutions to protect their human rights, additional justifications exist for ensuring that children's human rights are given special attention. These include the following facts: children's developmental state makes them particularly vulnerable to human rights violations; their opinions are still rarely taken into account; most children have no vote and cannot play a meaningful role in the political process that determines Governments' response to human rights; children encounter significant problems in using the judicial system to protect their rights or to seek remedies for violations of their rights; and children's access to organizations that may protect their rights is generally limited.[55]

40. The instrumental value of these rights is to construe citizens rather than mere consumers. It is to involve individuals as active participants in society – to empower them with political education – in order to increase their belief in their ability to have an impact and raise their level of responsibility.

---

[52] *Cf.* Article 3 of Protocol 1 to the ECHR which states: 'The High Contracting Parties undertake to hold free elections at reasonable intervals by secret ballot, under conditions, which will ensure the free expression of the opinion of the people in the choice of legislature'.

[53] CRC Committee, *Concluding Observations: Turkey* (UN Doc. CRC/C/15/Add.152, 2001), paras. 37–38.

[54] CRC Committee, *Concluding Observations: Republic of Korea* (UN Doc. CRC/C/15/Add.197, 2003), paras. 36–37. *Cf.* CRC Committee, *Concluding Observations: Cambodia* (UN Doc. CRC/C/15/Add.128, 2000).

[55] CRC Committee, *General Comment No 2 (2002) The role of independent national human rights institutions in the promotion and protection of the rights of the child, o.c.* (note 4), para. 5.

2. Article 13: The right to Freedom of Expression

41. The right contained in this provision is neither absolute nor non-derogable. The wording of Article 13 of the CRC is broad and it follows that of Article 19(2) and (3) of the CCPR, guaranteeing children and adolescents, the right to freedom of expression, encompassing the 'freedom to seek, receive, and impart information and ideas of all kinds'. The different components protected under Article 13(1) form an almost coherent whole. The right to *seek* is the active component and the tool to become informed. The right to *receive* is to an extent the passive component and its substantial meaning in jurisprudence has to an extent come to indicate a claim on the recipient's behalf on the media and hence authorities to guarantee that the public is informed on all matters of legitimate concern.[56] The right to *impart*, finally, is the active phase of the whole process; the way individuals express themselves, make their opinions known and have an impact in the world surrounding them. Freedom of opinion, which is protected separately and absolutely in Article 19(1) of the CCPR is omitted from Article 13(1). The question must hence be posed whether the textual omission is critical to the child's enjoyment of this right.

2.1 The de facto Recognition of Freedom of Opinion

42. From the discussions of the working groups during the drafting of the CRC it seems that the essence of the problem of freedom of opinion was bypassed or not given the consideration as was the case during the drafting of Article 19 of the CCPR. Opinion as an essential prerequisite for having an attitude or outlook is not protected explicitly as in the widely accepted human rights instruments, in particular the CCPR and the ECHR. The protection of views in Article 12(1) of the CRC concerns the protection of the right of children to be heard[57] in decision-making affecting them in particular in judicial and administrative proceedings when courts, welfare institutions or administrative authorities deal with children (*Cf.* Article 12(2)). The views of children must be given due weight and be taken seriously.[58]

---

[56] *Cf.* H. Thorgeirsdóttir, *o.c.* (note 26), p. 116.

[57] Press Release HR/4537, 11/06/2001. http://www.un.org/News/Press/docs/2001/hr4537.doc.htm.

[58] CRC Committee, *Concluding Observations: Albania* (UN Doc. CRC/C/15/Add.249, 2005), paras. 30–31. The CRC Committee further encouraged 'the State party to provide educational information to parents, teachers and headmasters, government administrative officials, the judiciary, children themselves and society at large with a view to creating an encouraging

Some State reports with regard to this right have stated that children after having reached a particular age have the right to reject an adoption or change of name or nationality.[59] 'Views' in Article 12 applies to the child's sentiments and outlooks and emphasizes its right to express them. There is a closer affinity between the child's guarantee to express its views in Article 12 CRC and the right to impart ideas of all kinds in Article 13(1) then an affinity with the protection of the process of forming an opinion, a process which is conditioned on freedom of information and communication by granting the child the freedom to form an opinion without interference as Article 19(1) of the CCPR does – the process necessary for becoming a mature participant in civil society.

43. Freedom of opinion from a contextual perspective is perhaps the most pivotal, consequential and vulnerable in the category of civil and political rights. To a degree it may be asserted that the other rights of expressing views, receiving and imparting information and ideas are only a means of realizing freedom of opinion.[60] It is hence surprising that this aspect of freedom of expression is not protected explicitly as opinion is distinct from thought and conscience protected in Article 14 of the CRC as a distinct freedom just like thought is a distinct freedom from opinion and expression in both the CCPR and ECHR.

44. The CRC *travaux préparatoires* do not reveal why paragraph 1 of Article 19 of the CCPR was not adopted like the rest of the article. It seems more like an 'accident' then 'deliberate' that freedom of opinion was not included, although this was proposed by a group of States when Article 19 of the CCPR provided the model for this parallel provision in children's convention.[61]

45. A proposal submitted by the US on civil and political rights of the child[62] combined what eventually turned out to be two separate provisions (Articles 12 and 13). This proposal contained 'views' in the first sentence of the first

---

atmosphere in which children, including those below the age of 10 years, can freely express their views, and where, in turn, these are given due weight. The views of children must be given due weight and be taken seriously'.

[59] T. Hammarberg, 'Children', in: A. Eide, C. Krause and A. Rosas (eds.), *Economic, Social and Cultural Rights* (Dordrecht/Boston/London, Martinus Nijhoff Publishers, 2001), p. 358.

[60] G. Malinverni, 'Freedom of Information in the European Convention on Human Rights and in the International Covenant on Civil and Political Rights', *Human Rights Law Journal* 4, No. 4, 1983, p. 445.

[61] S. Detrick, *o.c.* (note 16), p. 234, para. 44.

[62] *Travaux Préparatoires* (UN Doc. E/CN.4/1988/WG.1/WP. 18, 1988). *Cf.* also S. Detrick, *o.c.* (note 16), p. 232.

paragraph and the freedom to express them, adding in the next sentence that this right should include the right to seek, receive and impart information and ideas of all kinds, regardless of frontiers and form of expression.

46. Although the communist or socialist States at the time were sceptical of the emphasis on civil and political rights for the child, the majority supported the idea, albeit emphasizing the legitimate rights of parents, the balance between rights of children and parents and that the wording of the freedom of expression provision should be in line with Article 19 of the CCPR. There was apprehension of ideas to add a sentence protecting children from the interference of parents which led the Finnish observant to suggest a compromise allowing the child to express an opinion instead of the child's freedom of opinion. There was genuine apprehension of granting a guarantee to children to hold their own, independent opinions.[63]

47. A few States, among them the US and Finland, wanted to keep the provision parallel to Article 19(1), adding a paragraph (4) to safeguard the rights and duties to parents (or legal guardians) 'to provide direction to the child in the exercise of this rights in a manner consistent with the evolving capacities of the child'.[64]

Without any further explanations the working group reached a consensus deleting the guarantee to hold opinions and hence deleting the guarantee to safeguard parental guidance.

48. The only suggestion which may be seen as a gesture to protect the opinion formation process came from the delegation of the German Democratic Republic and it was to add the following phrase to the restriction clause 2 b (amendments emphasized): 'for the protection of national security or of public order (*ordre public*), or of public health or morals, *or the spiritual and moral well-being of the child*'.[65] The purpose according to the East German delegation was to cover certain dangers of violent information disseminated by the mass media.

49. The political or ideological conflict characteristic of the Cold War was obvious as the Chinese representative declared her support for the

---

[63] *Cf.* China and Morocco. *Travaux Préparatoires* (UN Doc. E/CN.4/1988/WG.1/WP. 18). *Cf.* also S. Detrick, *o.c.* (note 16), p. 234.

[64] *Travaux Préparatoires* (UN Doc. E/CN.4/1988/28, 1988). *Cf.* also S. Detrick, *o.c.* (note 16), pp. 234–235.

[65] *Travaux Préparatoires* (UN Doc. E/CN.4/1989/WG.1/WP.2., 1989). *Cf.* also S. Detrick, *o.c.* (note 16), pp. 234–235.

amendment while the delegate of the US regarded this addition as an extra restriction on freedom of expression. It is well conceivable that the mutual suspicion reflected in this debate may from the standpoint of States of free market liberalism be seen as not only reflecting 'paternalistic flavour of the amendment [was] against the spirit of the Convention'[66] but also as restricting the activities of media corporations of all kinds, imposing duties on them and making authorities liable. The Muslim countries as well as the communist States may on the other hand have seen it as a grave threat guaranteeing children under public international law the right to hold opinions absolutely. Such a guarantee might, in their perception, have paved the way for propaganda of market and consumer values, infiltrating the minds of adolescents with for example ideas antithetical to Islam. This is the most likely reason for excluding the important guarantee of freedom of opinion – the realisation that the inclusion of an absolute freedom of opinion would make the battle for young minds more pervasive.

50. Despite the omission of 'freedom of opinion' in the text of Article 13, the need to protect the delicate process of forming an opinion is evident in the emphasis of the CRC Committee concluding observations on State reports where the process of the child's forming of opinion is of major concern. The right to receive in addition to the right to seek also confirms that the child does not only need protection against harmful information but that she/he is also entitled to adequate and appropriate information to form the basis of the child's 'moral motivation'.[67] The recognition of this entitlement to appropriate and adequate information is in congruity with the instrumental value of this right in enlightening the individual (Cf. infra No. 35 et seq.).

51. It may hence be reasoned that the right to freedom of opinion is implied in Article 13(1), which is furthermore confirmed in the emphasis on the impact of harmful information on the minds of children (Cf. Infra No. 80 et seq.). The CRC Committee stated in a recent concluding observation on the Democratic People's Republic of Korea its concern about 'the lack of information on civil and political rights and persistent reports of limitations on the civil and political rights of citizens, including children, in particular freedoms of opinion, expression, thought, conscience, religion, and movement, as well as the right to privacy, as stated by the Commission on Human

---

[66] Ibid.
[67] Cf. J. Rawls, Political Liberalism (New York, Columbia University, 1996), p. 81.

Rights in its resolutions 2003/10 and 2004/13. The CRC Committee has emphasized that States undertake measures to promote the participation of children in social life, 'as well as the effective enjoyment of their fundamental freedoms, including the freedom of opinion, expression, and association'.[68]

52. A working group on children and the media in a report to the CRC Committee emphasized the need for action in the furtherance of media literacy.[69] The Working Group discussed the importance of helping children to become critical consumers of media in all its forms, a task which today fewer parents assume and which, although included in school curricula in some parts of the world, is not consistently or widely undertaken or implemented with updated information. This recommendation confirms the essential aspect of forming an opinion with a critical mind.

2.2   The Active Right to Seek Information

53. The right to know is an integral aspect of freedom of expression[70] as it allows the public to have an adequate view of, and to form a critical opinion on, the state of the society in which they live and on the authorities that govern them, whilst encouraging informed participation by the public in matters of common interest.[71] Guaranteeing the information flow in the international instruments is, firstly, recognition of a positive obligation implicit in the structural role of this right. Secondly, the antecedent assumption of the valuable role of freedom of expression and the media in democracy in enhancing the public debate is rendering the discourse meaningful with relevant information and ideas. If democracy is to survive, its livelihood depends on an informed citizenry. *Mutatis mutandis* if democracy has a future, the youth must be enlightened. James Madison realized this. His famous words in 1822 could equally describe the underlying presumptions of the information society:

> 'A popular government without popular information, or the means of acquiring it, is but a Prologue to Farce or a Tragedy, or perhaps both. Knowledge

---

[68] CRC Committee, *Concluding Observations: Nicaragua* (UN Doc. CRC/C/15/Add.108, 1999), para. 28.

[69] *Cf.* CRC Committee, *Report of a Working Group on Children and the Media* (UN Doc. CRC/C/66, Annex IV, 1997).

[70] E. Barendt, *Freedom of Speech* (Oxford, Clarendon Press, 1996), p. 82.

[71] *Cf.* Council of Europe, *Committee of Ministers Recommendation (2002) 2 to Member States on access to official documents* (Adopted by the Committee of Ministers on 21 February 2002 at the 784th meeting of the Ministers' Deputies).

will forever govern ignorance: And people who mean to be their own gover-
nors must *arm themselves with the power that knowledge gives.*'[72]

54. The debates on freedom of information that started in 1946 with the
aim of describing properly the essential features of the information process
and setting the international community's objectives continued on the
agenda of UNESCO as well as within the various organs of the CoE. The concept of freedom of information was replaced by the notion of 'free flow of
information' and 'free and balanced flow of information', which became one
of UNESCO's priorities in the mid-1970s. In 1978, a UNESCO international
commission, headed by Sean McBride, was handed the task of studying the
totality of communication problems in the modern world. The basic assumption of the commission's work published in a report was that informa-
tion/communication is a fundamental individual and collective right. It
endorsed the view that news is not a commercial commodity but a social
good with specific objectives.[73] The authors of Many Voices, One World
wrote:

> 'Communication nowadays, is a matter of human rights. But it is increasingly
> interpreted as the right to communicate, going beyond the right to receive
> communication or to be given communication. Communication is thus seen
> as a two way process, in which the partners – individual and collective – carry
> on a democratic and *balanced dialogue*, in contrast to monologue, is at the heart
> of much contemporary thinking, which is leading a process of developing a
> new area of social rights.'[74]

55. The freedoms to seek and receive fall into the category of 'freedom of
information' often also termed 'the right to know'. The right to seek focuses
on an inquiry initiated by the individual. The right to seek implies a correlative duty upon States to provide information to persons of legitimate
concern to them.[75] In many countries, freedom of information acts are based
on the twofold democratic claim, *e.g.* the right to be informed and the right
to have access to government and administration records.[76] Children in
Scotland have been granted the right to know in a special provision of the

---

[72] Quoted in. F. S. Haiman, *Speech and Law in a Free Society* (USA, University of Chicago
Press, 1981), p. 368. Emphasis added.

[73] UNESCO The McBride Report 1980, *Many Voices, One World* (Paris, UNESCO, 1980).

[74] *Ibid.*, p. 172.

[75] *Cf.* ECtHR, *Guerra* v. *Italy*, Judgment of 19 February 1998, *Reports* 1998, para. 53.

[76] M. Bullinger, 'Freedom of expression: an essential element of democracy', Report pre-
sented to the Sixth International Colloquy about the European Convention on Human Rights,
Sevilla, 13–16 November 1985, *Human Rights Law Journal* 6, No. 2–4, 1985, p. 340.

Freedom of Information Act,[77] which requires that public authorities respond to all information requests they receive within 20 working days. The Act explicitly sets out a right of access to those aged 12 or over, but children below this age can also exercise this right, provided they have a 'general understanding' of what it means to do so.

56. Information has increasingly been viewed as a fundamental right, granting the public a right to access to information in public administration where authorities are not to consider that they own such information.[78] At the same time the concept of information is an immensely problematic one. The width of it requires that the precise meaning be defined concretely in the context of the relevant circumstances, proceeding from the principle that all types of information should be available to everyone.[79] The CRC was intended to have due regard to the current problems confronting children and access to information was mentioned early on.[80]

Article 10 of the ECHR does not, as does its counterpart, Article 19 of the CCPR, include the word 'seek' with the right to impart and receive. The right to seek may be interpreted as being implicit in the right to impart and receive information and the freedom to take notice of information and freedom to seek information and ideas, which can lead to the possible extension of the right to information, akin to information acts in domestic law.[81] The preparatory work of the ECHR suggests that it was not the intention to connect Article 10 to the right to access to information held by public authorities. There are divergent views on whether the ECHR jurisprudence allows one to draw the conclusion from Article 10 that it guarantees the right of access to public information,[82] but that interpretation has been advocated by legal authors since the early 1980s.[83] In a report for the CoE on the subject, Article 10 case-law on access to official information is seen as leading to an indirect fundamental right, dependant on the general

---

[77] Adopted in January 2005.

[78] *Cf.* Council of Europe, *Parliamentary Assembly, Resolution 1003 (1993) on the ethics of journalism.*

[79] *Cf.* UN Doc. E/CN.4/Sub.2/1992/9, 1992, p. 4.

[80] *Travaux Préparatoires* (UN Doc. E/CN.4/L.1468, 1979), pp. 60–61. *Cf. also* S. Detrick, *o.c.* (note 16), pp. 617–618.

[81] M. Bullinger, *l.c.* (note 76), p. 340.

[82] D. Voorhoof, *Critical perspectives on the scope and interpretation of Article 10 of the European Convention on Human Rights, Mass Media Files No. 10* (Strasbourg, Council of Europe Press, 1995).

[83] *Cf.* G. Malinverni, *l.c.* (note 60), p. 449.

accessibility of the information under domestic law.[84] Since the landmark decision in the *Sunday Times* case[85] in the late 1970s, the instrumental view towards the public's right to receive information has been well-established. The ECtHR has, however, been reluctant to recognize a positive obligation on States to provide information to individuals. Applicants that have sought to persuade the Court to find such an obligation in different contexts have not been successful.[86] The ECmHR held that the freedom to receive information guaranteed by Article 10(1) is primarily a freedom of access to general sources of information, which may not be restricted by positive action of the state.[87] In the *Guerra* case in 1998, the Court rejected the applicability of Article 10,[88] although it acknowledged that 'public access to clear and full information . . . must be viewed as a basic human right'.[89] From the ECHR case-law it may be gathered that the State is not obliged to divulge information in certain circumstances.[90] According to the same reasoning, there might be other circumstances in which other types of official information come under the guarantee of Article 10.[91]

57. In *Gaskin* v. *United Kingdom*,[92] the applicant sought access to the case records regarding severe psychological problems he had experienced as a child. He had been taken into care at a very young age, after the death of his mother, and remained in care until he attained majority. Gaskin challenged the failure to grant him unimpeded access to information about his formative years. The ECtHR held there had been a breach of Article 8 of the ECRHR relating to private and family life, It rejected his claim, however, that Article 10(1) of the ECHR conferred on the individual a right of access to a register containing information on his personal position. It held that the right to freedom to receive information basically prohibited a government from restricting a person from receiving information others wished or were willing to impart to him.

---

[84] Council of Europe, Steering Committee on the Mass Media, *Study on access to official information*, Strasbourg 15 April 1995, CDMM (95) 15 Def., p. 39.

[85] ECtHR, *Sunday Times* v. *the United Kingdom*, Judgment of 26 April 1979, *Publications of the Court*, Series A, 30.

[86] *Cf.* A. Mowbray, *The Development of Positive Obligations under the European Convention on Human Rights by the European Court of Human Rights* (Oxford, Hart Publishing, 2004), p. 192.

[87] ECmHR, No. 10392/83, *Z* v. *Austria*, Decision of 13 April 1988, DR 56, p. 238.

[88] ECtHR, *Guerra* v. *Italy*, Judgment of 19 February 1998, *Reports* 1998, p. 210.

[89] *Ibid.*, para 34.

[90] *Cf.* ECtHR, *Leander* v. *Sweden*, Judgment of 26 March 1987, Series A, 16 and ECtHR, *Gaskin* v. *the United Kingdom*, Judgment of 7 August 1989, Series A, 160, para. 49.

[91] *Cf.* D. Voorhoof, *o.c.* (note 82), p. 45.

[92] ECtHR, *Gaskin* v. *the United Kingdom*, Judgment of 7 August 1989, Series A, 160, para. 52.

58. There may be vital interests at stake for adopted children to learn who their birth parents are. The current law (2005) in England and Wales is that children under 18 have no legal right to know the identity of their birth parents. Once they reach 18 they have a right to apply to see their birth record and to use the Adoption Contact Register. The Register enables adopted people get contact details of birth relatives who have also registered. Evidence suggests that children often find it difficult to assert their rights. They suffer from low awareness among adults of their rights, and they often find it difficult to get access to information for themselves. The Federal Constitutional Court in Switzerland has tried several cases concerning access to files containing information on a child's biological parents. In so doing it has taken into account, inter alia, the personal freedom guaranteed by the Federal Constitution and the European Convention on Human Rights, and weighed up the interests involved. It has recalled the importance for the child to know his or her background and for the parents not to have to divulge their past. In a recent case[93] it concluded that adopted children who reach adulthood thus have the right to know who their biological parents are, and therefore the right to consult the masked entries in the register of births, marriages and deaths, regardless of any conflicting interests that may exist.

59. Article 7 of the CRC stipulates that a child has the right to be registered, to have a name, to acquire a nationality and, as far as possible, the right to know and be cared for by his or her parents. The term 'as far as possible' must not be taken as a legal limitation, but as a reference to facts that can hamper the enjoyment of certain rights. In a similar spirit, the Hague Convention on protection of children and co-operation in respect of inter-country adoption asks states to make sure that data concerning the parents are stored and that children have access to the information.

60. The ECtHR held by ten votes to seven in case against France[94] where it is legal for women to give birth anonymously, that an adopted woman's right under Article 8 had not been violated by the French law denying her information about her natural mother. Few countries have legislation comparable to that applicable in France, at least as regards the child's permanent inability to establish parental ties with the natural mother if she

---

[93] Switzerland / b) Federal Court / c) Second Civil Court / d) 06–12–2001 / e) 5A.15/2001 / f) M.W. and K.S. v. the Grisons Cantonal Court / g) Arrêts du Tribunal fédéral (Official Digest), 128 III 113 /

[94] ECtHR, No. 42326/98, *Odievre* v. *France*, Judgement of 13 February 2003, Reports 2003.

continues to keep her identity secret from the child she has brought into the world.

61. In this case the competing interests were those of the 38 year old woman who had been adopted after birth to receive information about her natural mother and siblings and the right of the mother not to reveal her identity. At stake in the Court's view was the right to life, superior to any other right – not merely the right to know as all other rights are about giving quality to that very life. The French law was seen as offering the mother an opportunity to give birth in conditions that are as safe as possible with the benefit of medical assistance and that she in turn has the right to anonymity without having to worry about future disclosure of the ties with her offspring that she had decided to give for adoption.

62. In a dissenting opinion seven Judges held that the French legislation did not strike a fair balance as it accepted that a mother's decision constituted an absolute defense being definitely binding on the child who has no legal means to challenge the mother's unilateral decision. The effect of the mother's absolute 'right of veto' is that the rights of the child, which are recognized in the general scheme of the Convention, are entirely neglected and forgotten.[95]

63. The dissenting Judges pointed to the fact that certain countries expressly recognize the right 'to know'. Thus, in Germany the right of everyone to know their origins was established as a fundamental right of the personality, based on the general right to dignity and free development.[96]

64. The CRC Committee after considering Canada's second report concluded in 2003 that Canada was not sufficiently guaranteeing adopted children's right to know as far as possible their biological parents.[97] CRC recommended that Canada 'consider amending its legislation to ensure that information about the date and place of birth of adopted children and their biological parents are preserved and made available to these children'.[98] The right to

---

[95] ECtHR, No. 42326/98, *Odievre* v. *France*, Judgement of 13 February 2003, joint dissenting opinion of Judges Wildhaber, Sir Nicolas Bratza, Bonello, Loucaides, Cabral Barreto, Tulkens and Pellonpää, para 7.

[96] *Ibid.*, para. 14.

[97] CRC Committee, *Sessional/Annual Report* (UN Doc. CRC/C/133), 14. January 2004, paras. 79–81.

[98] *Ibid.*, para. 80.

know one's biological origin finds root in the CRC's aforementioned Article 7 and Article 8 where States must respect the right of the child to preserve his or her identity, including name and family relations as recognized by law without unlawful interference.

65. The CRC Committee in its concluding observations on Albania[99] examined the guarantee under the Albanian Constitution which recognizes the right to information in general, whereas Article 35 grants everyone's right to become acquainted with the data collected about him, except for the cases provided by law and incorporates the right of the child to information, and to become acquainted with the data on his parents, which are available with the relevant bodies. The Albanian law addresses the issue of information in two cases: the adoption of minors, and the child's placement in an orphanage. The CRC Committee pointed out that there is a vacuum in the legislative acts on the practical ways to implement this right for children, as noted by the State Party in its report. Furthermore, the Committee was concerned that the prevailing attitudes in the family, in school, in other institutions and in society at large were not conducive to the enjoyment of this right.[100] The CRC Committee encouraged the State Party to take all appropriate measures, including legal means, to fully implement Article 13, and to introduce measures to promote and guarantee the right of the child to freedom of expression.

66. In a 1981 recommendation on access to information held by public authorities, the CoE Committee of Ministers urged that the 'utmost endeavour should be made to ensure the fullest possible availability to the public of information held by public authorities'.[101] Information acts reflect that times are changing and that democratic procedures require more openness and transparency and not obsessive secrecy in deeply rooted elitism of those in power. The CoE Committee of Ministers in a recommendation in 2002[102]

---

[99] CRC Committee, *State party Report: Albania* (UN Doc. CRC/C/11/Add. 27, 2004), paras. 99–100.

[100] CRC Committee, *Concluding Observations: Albania* (UN Doc. CRC/C/15/Add. 249, 2005), paras. 36–37.

[101] Council of Europe, *Committee of Ministers Recommendation (81) 19 to Member States on the Access of Information held by Public Authorities.*

[102] Council of Europe, *Committee of Ministers Recommendation (2002) 2, o.c.* (note 71). Bearing in mind, in particular, Article 19 of the UDHR; Articles 6, 8 and 10 of the ECHR; the United Nations Convention on Access to Information; Public Participation in Decision-making and Access to Justice in Environmental Matters (adopted in Aarhus, Denmark, on 25 June 1998) and the Convention for the Protection of Individuals with regard to Automatic Processing of Personal Data of 28 January 1981 (ETS No. 108); the Declaration on the freedom of expression

urged that Member States should guarantee the right of everyone to have access, on request, to official documents held by public authorities. This principle should apply without discrimination on any ground, including that of national origin. Member States may limit the right of access to official documents. Limitations should be set down precisely in law, be necessary in a democratic society and be proportionate to the aim of protecting *inter alia*: national security, the prevention, investigation and prosecution of criminal activities; privacy and other legitimate private interests; commercial and other economic interests, be they private or public; the equality of parties concerning court proceedings; nature; inspection, control and supervision by public authorities; the economic, monetary and exchange rate policies of the state; the confidentiality of deliberations within or between public authorities during the internal preparation of a matter. Access to a document may be refused if the disclosure of the information contained in the official document would or would be likely to harm any of the interests mentioned in paragraph 1, unless there is an overriding public interest in disclosure. Accordingly, a public authority should, at its own initiative and where appropriate, take the necessary measures to make public information which it holds when such information is in the interest of promoting transparency of public administration and/or encourage informed participation by the public in matters of public interest.[103] After adopting Resolution (2000) 2 on the CoE's information strategy, the Committee of Ministers has adopted a new policy on access to its own documents, based on the principle that 'transparency is the rule and confidentiality the exception'.

67. Article 19, the International Centre Against Censorship in London, has elaborated nine principles on 'Freedom of Information Legislation' to epitomize the ways in which governments can achieve maximum openness, in line with the best international standards and practice.[104] According to

---

and information adopted on 29 April 1982; as well as Recommendation No. R (81) 19 on the access to information held by public authorities, Recommendation No. R (91) 10 on the communication to third parties of personal data held by public bodies; Recommendation No. R (97) 18 concerning the protection of personal data collected and processed for statistical purposes and Recommendation No. R (2000) 13 on a European policy on access to archives.

[103] Council of Europe Committee of Ministers (2002) 8, Steering Committee for Human Rights (CDDH) a. Abridged report of the 52nd meeting (Strasbourg, 6 9 November 2001) b. Draft Recommendation Rec (2002) of the Committee of Ministers to member states on the access to official information

[104] These principles were drafted by Toby Mendel, Head of Article 19's Law Programme. They are the product of a long process of study, analysis and consultation overseen by Article 19 and drawing on extensive experience and work with partner organizations in many countries around the world.

Article 19 principle 1, 'information' and 'public bodies' should be defined broadly. Private bodies should be included if they hold information whose disclosure is likely to diminish the risk of harm to key public interests, such as the environment and health. Given the considerable role that corporations play in modern societies, the demands for their openness, transparency and accountability are growing. It is recommended in the above Article 19 principles that the destruction of records be a criminal offence.

68. The right to seek implies that authorities must guarantee children as well as adults equal opportunities in accessing information (*Cf. infra* No. 76). With regard to the scope of discrimination in the CCPR, Nowak notes, 'In the final analysis, every conceivable distinction that cannot be objectively justified is an impermissible discrimination.'[105]

69. The right to seek information of 'all kinds' and form of the child's choice may provide scope for seeking access to violent, vulgar or pornographic material. A recent observation of the CRC Committee concerned the easy access that children have to pornographic DVDs sold locally.[106] The CRC Committee recommended in light of Article 17(e) (which encourages the development of appropriate guidelines for the protection of the child from information and material injurious to his or her well-being, bearing in mind the provision of Articles 13 and 18 (parental responsibility)) that the State Party take all necessary measures to protect children from exposure to harmful information, including pornography. The Committee further recommended that the State Party take into consideration the Committee's recommendations emanating from its day of general discussion on the child and the media.[107]

70. CRC jurisprudence clearly implies that States have positive obligations in protecting children from injurious material in exercising their right to seek information, as it is in the best interest of the child to take into account its vulnerability and protection needs in this process.[108] The right of children to know about their origin is also stronger in CRC jurisprudence[109] than

---

[105] M. Nowak, *U.N. Covenant on Civil and Political Rights—CCPR Commentary* (Kehl/Strasbourg/Arlington, N.P. Engel, 1993), p. 45.

[106] CRC Committee, *Concluding Observations: Sao Tome and Principe* (UN Doc. CRC/C/15/Add. 235, 2004), paras. 31–32.

[107] CRC Committee, *Day of General Discussion on the Child and the Media* (UN Doc. CRC/C/57, 1996), paras. 242–257.

[108] CRC General Comment No. 6, 2005

[109] http://www.canadiancrc.com/articles/Adoption_Canada_denies_birthright.htm

in the new case law of the ECtHR,[110] which has departed from its prior jurisprudence more in line with the instrumental value of the right to know as the basis of self-development. Children's right to know based on decisions on their behalf is expressly proclaimed in the CRC, *e.g.* Articles 7 and 8 taken in conjunction with Article 13.

2.3   The Right to Receive Information and Ideas of 'All Kinds'

71. 'The greatest menace to freedom is an inert people', said American Justice Louise Brandeis many decades ago, adding that 'public discussion is a political duty'.[111] There is more than a semantic difference between an 'informed public' and a 'public informed'.[112] An informed public is an 'enlightened public', which the European Court of Human Rights visualized in one of its most famous freedom of expression cases[113] in late 1970s while a public informed can be confined to being informed on some isolated incident without any democratic significance.[114] Enlightened children are a hope for the future. The most persuasive argument underlying this right is the democratic rationale; the right to receive demands that the public have access to 'those facts necessary for public judgment about public things, and, more important, that it have the greatest possible opportunity to learn and master the art of political judgment'.[115]

2.3.1   Adequate Information

72. There is an affinity between the right to receive in Article 13(1) and Article 28 of the CRC making it mandatory on States Parties to recognize the right of the child to education and with a view to achieving this right progressively and on the basis of equal opportunity.[116] Article 13 of the CRC

---

[110] *Cf.* ECtHR, No. 42326/98, *Odievre* v. *France*, Judgement of 13 February 2003, *Reports 2003*

[111] *Cf. Whitney* v. *California,* 274 US 357 (1927) at 372.

[112] Bathory and McWilliams, quoted in D. M. O'Brien, *The Public's Right to Know: The Supreme Court and the First Amendment* (USA, Praeger Publishers, 1981), p. 13.

[113] ECtHR, *Sunday Times* v. *the United Kingdom,* Judgment of 26 April 1979, *Publications of the Court,* Series A, 30, para. 65. The Court concluded, 'not only do the media have the task of imparting such information and ideas: the public also has a right to receive them'.

[114] The Court rejected the notion of raw journalism, imparting information without any analysis in ECtHR, *Lingens* v. *Austria,* Judgment of 8 July 1986, *Publications of the Court,* Series A, 103, para. 41.

[115] Bathory and McWilliams, *l.c.* (note 112), p. 13.

[116] See in general, M. Verheyde, 'Article 28: The Right to Education', in: A. Alen, J. Vande Lanotte, E. Verhellen, F. Ang, E. Berghmans and M. Verheyde (eds.), *A Commentary on the United Nations Convention on the Rights of the Child* (Leiden/Boston, Martinus Nijhoff Publishers, 2005), pp. 1–69.

must also be read in context with Article 29 of the CRC with regard to the child's right to receive emphasizing the authorities' responsibility in the direction of education which shall *inter alia* aim at the development of the child's personality, talents and mental and physical abilities to their fullest potential.[117] The CRC Committee has in this respect emphasized the need for professionals and voluntary workers involved in the education and protection of children to receive adequate training and education, taking into account the principles set forth in the Convention. The Committee also recommends that the Convention be included in the curricula of Catholic schools. In this respect, it is the view of the Committee that the teaching methods used in schools should reflect the spirit and philosophy of the Convention and the aims of education laid down in its Articles 28 and 29.[118]

73. A report from Eritrea stated that although the Constitution guarantees the right of access to information it had to be recognized that some children do not currently have access to adequate information, and in the longer term the Government is committed to change this situation (through education, organized activities or the media). It launched a new initiative of establishing community public libraries throughout the country.[119]

74. The right to receive implies that children must be treated on equal basis with regard to the enjoyment of any civil right. The CRC Committee pointed to the fact that a State Party had not taken all legal and other appropriate measures to promote and implement the rights contained in Articles 13, 14 and 15. Of particular concern is the fact that children considered poor are channelled towards monastic Buddhist schools and are offered no alternative educational opportunity. This might challenge the right to freedom of religion for non-Buddhist children who are enrolled in those schools. Deep concern was also expressed by the Committee with regard to the right of children to freedom of speech, association and peaceful assembly. Moreover, the Committee was seriously concerned by the recent closure of some high schools.[120]

---

[117] See in general, G. Alfredsson and K. Kondo, 'Article 29: The Aims of Education', in: A. Alen, J. Vande Lanotte, E. Verhellen, F. Ang, E. Berghmans and M. Verheyde (eds.), *A Commentary on the United Nations Convention on the Rights of the Child* (Leiden/Boston, Martinus Nijhoff Publishers, 2005).

[118] CRC Committee, *Concluding Observations: Holy Sea* (UN Doc. CRC/C/15/Add.46, 1995), para. 12. On participation in education, see also M. Verheyde, 'Article 28: The Right to Education', *l.c.* (note 116), pp. 57–59, No. 45.

[119] CRC Committee, *State Party Report: Eritrea* (UN Doc. CRC/C/41/Add.12, 2002), para. 128.

[120] CRC Committee, *Concluding Observations: Myanmar* (UN Doc. CRC/C/15/Add.69, 1997), para. 16. On equal access and opportunities opportunities in education, see also M. Verheyde, 'Article 28: The Right to Education', *l.c.* (note 116), pp. 36–46, No. 28–34.

75. The ECtHR has reiterated that the State has an obligation to secure to children their right to education (Article 2 of Protocol 1 to the ECHR)[121] and that the provision guaranteeing education must be read in conjunction Articles 8, 9 and 10 of the Convention, which proclaim the right of everyone, including parents and children, '"to respect for his private and family life", to "freedom of thought, conscience and religion", and to "freedom to receive and impart information and ideas"'.[122] The Court has furthermore emphasized that those responsible as representatives of the State must be mindful of the rights of children not to be exposed to influences which are hard to square with the principle of gender equality.[123]

76. Children may not be subject to any arbitrary discrimination in their right to adequate information. The UN Human Rights Committee in the case of *Diergardt v. Namibia* held that the lack of language legislation in Namibia violated Article 26 of the CCPR, which states that people are entitled to the equal protection of the law. The authors of the complaint claimed that the consequence of the lack of language legislation in Namibia was that they had been denied the use of their mother tongue in administration, justice, education and public life.[124] The circumstances of this case are particularly pertinent to the situation of children who are often less equipped to deal with the 'system' than grown ups and are habitually met with condescension when trying to seek assistance. In the case of Namibia, civil servants were instructed to use the English language – not Afrikaans – in contacts with the public, even on the phone when the civil servants could easily have responded in that language.[125] The decision in this case does not contradict the reasoning of the ECtHR in the *Belgian Linguistic* case.[126] It confirms that any language preference must not be arbitrary or unreasonable.

77. The CRC Committee recommended in the case of Kazakhstan which had reported[127] that the numbers of periodicals (magazines and newspapers),

---

[121] ECtHR, *Costello-Roberts* v. *the United Kingdom*, Judgment of 25 March 1993, *Publications of the Court*, Series A, 247, paras. 25–28.

[122] ECtHR, *Kjeldsen, Busk and Madsen* v. *Denmark*, 7 December 1976, *Publications of the Court*, Series A, 23, para. 52.

[123] *Cf.* ECtHR, No. 42393/98, *Dahlab* v. *Switzerland*, Decision of 15 February 2001, *Reports* 2001-V, p. 463.

[124] Human Rights Committee, *Diergaardt et al. v. Namibia*, Communication No. 760/1997, CCPR/C/69/D/760/1997, Decision of 6 December 2000.

[125] *Ibid.*

[126] ECtHR, *Belgian Linguistic Case*, Judgment of 23 July 1968, *Publications of the Court*, Series A, 6.

[127] CRC Committee, *State Party Report: Kazakhstan* (UN Doc. CRC/C/41/Add.13, 2002).

books and booklets published for children are declining (at the same time, commercial book publishing, primarily in Russian, facilitates access to classical literature, encyclopaedias and reference works, including those for children),[128] that the State Party take all effective measures, including enacting or reviewing legislation where necessary, to ensure that the child's freedom of expression and the right of access to information is guaranteed and implemented. In light of Articles 13 and 17 of the CRC, the Committee was concerned that the quality and quantity of printed information, including children's books, available to children had decreased in recent years, while at the same time there is a lack of mechanisms to protect children from information and material injurious to their well-being.[129]

78. In another case, the CRC Committee recommended that the State Party take appropriate measures to allow access to appropriate information from a diversity of sources, especially those aimed at the promotion of the child's social, spiritual and moral well-being and physical and mental health due to its concern that access to information and material from a diversity of national and international sources is very limited for persons under 18 years of age in the State Party. The Committee was further concerned at the little protection provided to children from viewing offensive and pornographic materials.[130]

79. The CRC Committee expressed its concern that children living in rural communities are particularly disadvantaged and have insufficient access to appropriate information.[131] It recommended that authorities in the Marshall Islands 'reinforce measures for the production of programmes and books for children and disseminate them within the country, in particular the outer islands, and in this regard envisage taking steps for the introduction of the use of computers in schools'.[132]

---

[128] *Ibid.*, para. 146.
[129] CRC Committee, *Concluding Observations: Kazakhstan* (UN Doc. CRC/C15/Add.213, 2003), paras. 34–35.
[130] CRC Committee, *Concluding Observations: Togo* (UN Doc. CRC/C/15/Add.255, 2005), paras. 40–41; *Mozambique* (UN Doc. CRC/C/83/Add.1, 2001), para. 35
[131] CRC Committee, *Concluding Observations: Mozambique* (UN Doc. CRC/C/83/Add.1, 2001), para. 35.
[132] CRC Committee, *Concluding Observations: Marshall Islands* (UN Doc. CRC/C/15/Add.139, 2000), paras. 34–35.

2.3.2 Appropriate Information

80. Children have a right to receive all kinds of information under Article 13(1). This freedom may be subject to restrictions under Article 13(2) for various reasons including rights of others and public health and morals. In most cases where the CRC Committee comments on the exercise of children's right to receive information under Article 13 and also Article 17 dealing with the mass media, it notes the urgent need to ensure adequate protection of children from harmful information, and particularly from television programmes inciting or containing violence.[133]

81. Article 17 of the CCPR expressly guarantees the right of an individual against unlawful attacks on his or her honour or reputation. Article 20 of the CCPR explicitly prohibits propaganda for war and advocacy for national, racial or religious hatred. Article 4 of the CERD declares that it is an offence punishable by law to disseminate ideas based on racial superiority or hatred. Article 10 of the ECHR does not in its text protect the dissemination of information and ideas of 'all kinds', which may indicate a more structured and instrumental approach to protection especially in light of the ECHR jurisprudence. The essence of protection of freedom of expression is reflected in one of the most famous phrases concerning Article 10:

> 'The Court's supervisory functions oblige it to pay the utmost attention to the principles characterizing a "democratic society". Freedom of expression constitutes one of the essential foundations of such a society, one of the basic conditions for its progress and for the development of every man. Subject to paragraph 2 of Article 10 (art. 10–2), it is applicable not only to 'information" or "ideas" that are favourably received or regarded as inoffensive or as a matter of indifference, but also to those that offend, shock or disturb the State or any sector of the population. Such are the demands of that pluralism, tolerance and broadmindedness without which there is no "democratic society".'[134]

82. In the case of *Handyside*,[135] the ECtHR dealt with matters concerning dissemination of sexual matters to youngsters. It submitted that the right of the State to intervene was enhanced because the material was aimed at children. In *Otto Preminger* v. *Austria* the ECtHR reiterated its general principles, stating *inter alia* that according to Article 10(2), whoever exercises

---

[133] CRC Committee, *Concluding Observations: Canada* (UN Doc. CRC/C/15/Add.37, 1995), para. 15.

[134] ECtHR, *Handyside v. the United Kingdom,* Judgment of 7 December 1976, *Publications of the Court,* Series A, 24, para. 49.

[135] *Ibid.*

the rights and freedoms in the first paragraph of that article undertakes 'duties and responsibilities'.[136] In this context the duties may legitimately include an obligation to avoid as far as possible expressions that are gratuitously offensive to others and thus an infringement of their rights, and which therefore do not contribute to any form of public debate capable of furthering progress in human affairs.[137] The ECtHR submitted that:

> 'It is somewhat artificial [. . .] to draw a rigid distinction between "protection of the rights and freedoms of others" and "protection of morals". The latter may imply safeguarding moral ethos or moral standards of a society as whole, but may also cover protection of moral interests and welfare of a particular section of society, for example schoolchildren. Thus, "protection of the rights and freedoms of others", when meaning the safeguarding of moral interests and welfare of certain individuals or classes of individuals who are in need of special protection for lack of maturity, mental disability or state of dependence, amounts to one aspect of "protection of morals".'[138]

83. With regard to harmful information, the CRC Committee has recommended that authorities continue and strengthen efforts to ensure that all children have access to appropriate information. In the case of Luxembourg, the CRC Committee recommended that the State Party continue to take all appropriate measures to effectively protect children from being exposed to violence, racism and pornography through mobile technology, video movies, games and other technologies, including the Internet. The CRC Committee further suggested that the State Party develop programmes and strategies to use mobile technology, video advertisements and the Internet as a means for raising awareness among both children and parents of information and material injurious to the well-being of children.[139]

84. In 1998, the CoE Parliamentary Assembly emphasized that children need to be protected from harmful media content as today's citizens and they have the right to quality media as tomorrow's society-caretakers.[140] Noting

---

[136] ECtHR, *Otto-Preminger Institute* v. *Austria*, Judgement of 20 September 1994, *Publications of the Court*, Series A, 295, para. 49.

[137] ECtHR, *Dudgeon* v. *Ireland*, 22 October 1981, *Publications of the Court*, Series A, 45, para. 47.

[138] CRC Committee, *Concluding Observations: Luxembourg* (UN Doc. CRC/C/15/Add.250, 2005), paras. 30–31.

[139] Council of Europe, *Parliamentary Assembly Recommendation 1371(1998) on the abuse and neglect of children*.

[140] Council of Europe *Parliamentary Assembly Recommendation 963 (1983) on cultural and educational means of reducing violence*.

the need to promote from early childhood onwards a policy of equality between girls and boys, and women and men, the media is encouraged to place greater emphasis on the production of information and educational programmes seeking to promote the participation of children in family and social life. The CoE Parliamentary Assembly has asked Member States to take appropriate measures to ensure that broadcasting companies give particular attention to means of protecting sensitive people, especially children from prolonged media violence and expressed concern that artistic freedom should not be used as an alibi for purely commercial interests.[141] The ECtHR has held that the rights of the holder of parental authority (schools) are not unlimited and that the State must provide safeguards against abuse.[142] Children are widely exposed to violent, vile and stupefying material on television in their homes. This is a fact known in most households although the broadcasting companies cannot in virtue of the 'in loco parentis' doctrine be held responsible. The authorities in the CoE Member States on the other hand, have an obligation under Article 1 of the ECHR as frequently reiterated to secure that children, even within their homes, are not exposed to treatment contrary to Article 3 of the ECHR.[143] The ECtHR has referred to the CRC to illustrate the responsibility of the State where children's dignity is concerned.[144]

85. Imposing 'obscene' material on those who cannot oppose it is according to Emerson and McKinnon a form of physical assault.[145] A child exposed to violence in the form of vulgar covers on magazines or obscene sexual programmes on television has his moral integrity invaded and is also suffering an attack on his moral integrity and in the case of the television in the sanctity of the home,[146] as the concept of private life in the ECHR case-law covers physical and moral integrity.[147] According to ECHR jurisprudence

---

[141] ECtHR, *Costello-Roberts* v. *the United Kingdom*, Judgment of 25 March 1993, *Publications of the Court*, Series A, 247, para. 28.

[142] *Cf.* ECmHR, *Costello-Roberts* v. *the United Kingdom*, Report 8 October 1991, *Publications of the Court*, Series A, para. 37.

[143] ECtHR, *Costello-Roberts* v. *the United Kingdom*, Judgment of 25 March 1993, *Publications of the Court*, Series A, 247, para. 27.

[144] *Cf.* C.A. MacKinnon, *Only Words* (Cambridge, Mass., Harvard University Press, 1993), p. 108.

[145] ECtHR, *Costello-Roberts* v. *the United Kingdom*, Judgment of 25 March 1993, *Publications of the Court*, Series A, 247, para. 34.

[146] ECtHR, *X and Y* v. *the Netherlands*, Judgement of 26 March 1985, *Publications of the Court*, Series A, 91, paras. 22–27.

[147] *Ibid.*, para. 23; ECtHR, *Airey* v. *Ireland*, 9 October 1979, *Publications of the Court*, Series A, 32, para. 32.

with regard to Article 8, the State may have a positive obligation in protecting individuals, in this context, from media conduct that does not take into account their moral integrity.[148]

86. In the *Müller* case, the ECtHR took into consideration the 'violent reaction' of a young girl exposed to paintings in an art gallery in the attendance of her father. The paintings depicted in a crude manner sexual relations between men and animals. The government in Switzerland contended that the aim of the interference of the freedom of expression of the artist was to protect the morals and the rights of others, relying above all on the reaction of a man and his daughter. On the basis of an implicit value judgment of the Swiss judges' attitudes about morality, the ECtHR held that the necessity test had been met and the measures adopted were proportional.[149] The ECtHR emphasized freedom of artistic expression maintaining that those who create, perform and distribute works of art, contribute to the exchange of ideas and opinions, which is essential for democratic society. Hence the obligation on the State not to encroach unduly on their freedom of expression.[150] In justifying the restriction, the ECtHR referred to the heightened responsibility of those exercising this right in proportion to their influence and impact on others, saying that whoever exercises this freedom is not immune to limitations as provided for in Article 10(2). In accordance with the express terms of that paragraph, the scope of 'duties and responsibilities' of the holder of the right depends on the situation and the means he uses.[151] Referring to *Handyside* the ECtHR placed the burden of 'duties and responsibilities' on private individuals using means, which could reach the morally sensitive, young people at a critical stage of their development. In Handyside it held that adolescents could have interpreted the material as an encouragement to indulge in precocious activities harmful for them or even to commit certain criminal offences.[152] Restrictions of such material are hence conducive to the protection of morals necessary in a democratic society.[153]

---

[148] *Cf.* St. J. MacDonald, 'The Margin of Appreciation' in: MacDonald et al. (ed.), *The European System for the Protection of Human Rights* (The Netherlands, Kluwer Law International, 1993), p. 89.

[149] ECtHR, *Müller and Others v. Switzerland*, Judgment of 24 May 1998, *Publications of the Court*, Series A, 133, para. 33.

[150] *Ibid.*, para. 34.

[151] ECtHR, *Handyside v. the United Kingdom*, Judgment of 7 December 1976, *Publications of the Court*, Series A, 24, para. 52.

[152] *Ibid.*, para. 52.

[153] ECtHR, *Handyside v. the United Kingdom*, Judgment of 7 December 1976, *Publications of the Court*, Series A, 24, para. 62.

Confiscation of pornographic literature and other material forbidden by law does not violate property rights under the ECHR if considered to be in the general interest.[154]

2.3.3 Children and the Internet

87. In a comment on the situation in Uzbekistan, the CRC Committee expressed its concern that in the light of Article 13 (the child's right to seek, receive and impart information) and Article 17 of the Convention (the right of access to information, including information and material from a diversity of cultural, national and international sources), that stringent registration and licensing requirements for the media and publications, as well as restrictions on Internet access, did not comply with Article 13(2) of the CRC.[155]

88. Article 17 of the CRC deals with the function of the mass media.[156] The media, broadly defined, also have a central role to play, both in promoting the values and aims reflected in Article 29(1) of the CRC and in ensuring that their activities do not undermine the efforts of others to promote those objectives. Governments are obligated by the Convention, pursuant to article 17(a), to take all appropriate steps to 'encourage the mass media to disseminate information and material of social and cultural benefit to the child'.[157] The principle of free flow of information across frontiers is adopted in the European Convention on Transfrontier Television of 1989 and the EC Directive on Television without Frontiers from the same time.[158] Both instruments formulate the same fundamental principle that reception of broadcasts emanating from Member States must be allowed in other jurisdictions, provided they comply with common standards for programmes and advertising. The restriction clauses of the articles protecting the information flow in the CCPR, the ECHR and the CRC may, however, provide a basis for a prior consent principle of the recipient State, as a State must ensure that

---

[154] CRC Committee, *Concluding Observations: Uzbekistan* (UN Doc. CRC/C/15/Add.167, 2001), para. 37.

[155] ECtHR, *X, Y and Z v. the United Kingdom,* Judgment of 20 March 1997, *Reports 1997-IV.* Judge Pettiti submitted in a concurring opinion, that the Court should take into consideration the interests of children and to give priority to the interests of the child in complex situations of modern life – with regard to Article 8 to protect family life.

[156] CRC Committee, *General Comment No. 1: The Aims of Education, Article 29(1)* (UN Doc. CRC/GC/2001/1, 2001), para. 21.

[157] ETS 132, 1989, p. 243.

[158] The CRC Committee includes it in the category of media in its general discussion on the Child and the Media: CRC Committee, *Day of General Discussion on the Child and the Media* (UN Doc. CRC/C/57, 1996), paras. 242–257.

foreign broadcasts do not conflict with the vital interests such as national security, health and morals.

89. With regard to the Internet,[159] the ECtHR has held that Article 10 applies not only to the content of information but 'also to the means of transmission or reception since any restriction imposed on the means necessarily interferes with the right to receive and impart information'.[160] The world wide web (www) contains a tremendous amount of information contained in millions of web pages. The Internet is the first medium where global distribution is inevitable. The right to receive information under Article 13 of the CRC is regardless of frontiers. This worldwide computer network gives rise to new legal issues, especially in public international law, particularly on freedom of expression, discriminatory content, pornography, paedophilia and racism, violence and crime, the rights of the child, universal access, intellectual property and fair use, protection of privacy, personal data security and the overall objectives of promoting democracy by contributing to pluralism, tolerance and broadmindedness and protecting individual dignity. Attempts to control the Internet, which has no physical existence, no centralized storage location or control point linking individuals, corporations and governments around the world seem futile. It is out of the reach of a single entity to regulate the information conveyed on the Internet.[161]

90. The Internet has enormous potential for disseminating hate propaganda, pornography and paedophilia,[162] as has been recognized by the CRC Committee.[163] It is hence a powerful *means* with regard to children having access to harmful information. The CRC Committee has encouraged States Parties to ratify the Optional Protocol to the CRC on the sale of children, child prostitution and child pornography.[164] From the perspective of the

---

[159] ECtHR, *Autronic AG v. Switzerland*, Judgment of 22 May 1990, *Publications of the Court*, Series A, 178, para. 47.

[160] R. Wacks, 'Privacy in Cyberspace: Personal Information, Free Speech and the Internet' in: P. Birks (ed.) *Privacy and Loyalty* (United Kingdom, Clarendon Press, 1997), pp. 93, 95–96, 97, 102. *Cf.* H. Thorgeirsdóttir, *o.c.* (note 26), p. 133.

[161] *Cf.* Council of Europe, *Committee of Ministers Recommendation (2001) 16 on the protection of children against sexual exploitation* (Adopted by the Committee of Ministers on 31 October 2001 at the 771st meeting of the Ministers' Deputies).

[162] CRC Committee, *Concluding Observations: Monaco* (UN Doc. CRC/C/15/Add.158, 2001), paras. 28–29.

[163] CRC Committee, *Concluding Observations: Belgium* (UN Doc. CRC/C/15/Add.178, 2002), para. 33. *Cf.* Optional Protocol to the Convention on the Rights of the Child and the sale of children, child prostitution and child pornography. Adopted and opened for signature, ratification and accession by General Assembly resolution A/Res/54/263 of 25 May 2000; entered into force on 18 January 2002. Ratified by 85 States (as at November 2004).

[164] *Cf.* CRC Committee, *Concluding Observations: Nicaragua* (UN Doc. CRC/C/15/Add.36, 1995), para. 34.

child its right to privacy needs to be reinforced.[165] There is wide consensus that illegal online communications which cover violent pornography, organized crime, terrorism, racism or hate-speech should be subject to law enforcement, although there is no agreement on how this would be done. In John Stuart Mill's theory on liberty, the only part of the conduct of anyone, for which he is amenable to society, is that which concerns others. Immune from this principle are children and young persons below the age which the law may fix as that of manhood or womanhood. They need protection against external injury.[166]

91. It is also disputed how far regulation on the Internet might go without compromising freedom of expression. Some freedom of expression scholars use the word 'sexual material' instead of 'pornography' to emphasize what in their view constitutes censorship, *i.e.* the need to exert control over what others read and think and claim that there is a difference between children with regard to whether they are 17 or 10 year old and basically that what is considered 'harmful' or 'inappropriate' is culture driven; and that there is furthermore little evidence on harmful or traumatic effects.[167] Strossen points out that the term 'pornography' has no legal significance in the US Supreme Court's First Amendment jurisprudence: 'While the Court has upheld two statutes[168] that prohibited what each defined as "child pornography", the Court has not itself defined a constitutionally unprotected category of "child pornography." Both State statutes defined the prohibited expression relatively narrowly, as encompassing photographs or films that show actual children either engaging in sexual activities or in a state of nudity.'[169]

92. Understandably many parents worry about their children's exposure to vulgarity on the Internet. The problem of the harmful impact is, however,

---

[165] J.S. Mill, *On Liberty*, (New York: Bantham Books, 1993), p. 13. Mill, for the same reason, thought it essential to protect the 'backward stages of society in which the race itself may be considered in its non age'(around the middle of the 19th century). Mill thought that tyranny was a legitimate mode of government in dealing with barbarians (uncultured or uncivilized persons), 'provided the end be their improvement, and the means justified by actually effecting that end'.

[166] *Cf.* M. Heins, *Not in Front of the Children: Indecency, Censorship and the Innocence of Youth* (USA, Hill and Wang, 2001).

[167] *Cf.* N. Strossen, *Defending Pornography: Free Speech, Sex and the Fight for Women's Rights* (New York University Press, 2000). Referring to *New York v. Ferber*, 458 US 747 (1982); *Osborne v. Ohio*, 495 US 103 (1990).

[168] *Ibid.*, p. 59.

[169] IP/01/1392, 10 October 2001.

not a concern of the majority of the world's children since they do not have access to the Internet. Wide differences (between 'haves' and 'have-nots') remain in Internet use in schools within the European Union.[170] In the world wide context there is, however, undeniably a huge digital divide in other countries and continents between the 'haves' and the 'have-nots'. Lack of access to information poses a global threat to children in countries like China where it has been estimated that over 60 percent of the total Chinese population living in predominantly rural areas has access to only 0.8 per cent of total Internet connections. [171] With information and communication technology such an integral part of education, this digital divide will impact heavily on the development potentials of children who do not have access to the Internet. This situation speaks clearly of the interrelation between civil and political rights on the one hand and economic and social rights on the other hand.

93. With regard to the children who do not have access to the Internet, the concerns in the late 1940s of one principal drafters of the ECHR, Pierre Henri Teitgen, are still relevant. In the aftermath of World War II, the economies of the European continent were ruined; millions were homeless and hungry and hence like raising false expectations when speaking of the enjoyment of civil freedoms when people were on the brink of starvation. The worries of this wise man are of no less relevance in today's global context where hundred of millions of poor children,[172] whose governments have ratified the CRC, have no chance of enjoying their right to freedom of expression given the economic and social conditions in their countries. Professor Teitgen when referring to Western Europe, where millions still lacked the means to exercise the fundamental freedoms, stated:[173]

> 'It is true that these freedoms are written into the laws; they exist on papers for them as for others, the privileged ones; but those poverty-stricken creatures lack the means to exercise them and to benefit by them day by day . . . Of what value is the principle of free access to public appointments, if, in practice, education, culture, and humanism are the privilege of inherited wealth?'

---

[170] *Cf.* 'The Digital Divide in China': Can also be consulted at: http://www.unicef.org/china/media_1164.html

[171] *Cf. ibid.:* Poverty, armed conflict and HIV/Aids threaten their survival and development.

[172] Collected edition of the *Travaux Préparatories*, Vol. 1 (The Netherlands, Kluwer Law International, 1975), Introduction and p. 42.

[173] Loyal opposition is the concept that one can be opposed to the actions of the government of the day without being opposed to the constitution of the political system.

2.4   *The Right to Impart and Political Dissent*

94. Freedom of expression under CRC as well as the CCPR and ACHR entails the right to impart information and ideas of all kinds while Article 10 of the ECHR omits 'all kinds' but adds without public interference. Speaking of children's right to impart in light of the participatory nature of their freedom of expression and the democratic context, it must be taken into account that democratic culture allowing loyal opposition[174] is not prevailing in many of the contracting parties to the CRC. The Inter-American Commission on Human Rights in a report on Cuba underscores that citizens are allowed freedom of speech and press in accordance with the Constitution, which subordinates the exercise of freedom of expression to 'the purpose of the communist society.' This means that it is not the State whose action is limited *vis-á-vis* the rights of persons, but on the contrary, persons' rights are limited *vis-á-vis* the purposes pursued by the state.[175]

95. The CRC Committee has expressed its concern at the lack of legal guarantees for the freedom of expression for children below 18 years of age, with regard to the inadequate attention given to the promotion of and respect for the right of the child to freedom of expression, and that prevailing traditional societal attitudes, in the family and in other settings regarding the role of children, appear to make it difficult for children to seek and impart information freely. In such cases, the CRC Committee has recommended that States take all appropriate measures, including amendments to legislation, to promote and guarantee the right of the child to freedom of expression within the family, in the school and other institutions and in society.[176]

96. Harry Kalven, a notable writer on the law of free speech said, 'society can, for example, either treat obscenity as a crime or not a crime without thereby altering its basic nature as a society'.[177] A society, however, that does not tolerate political dissent, defines itself as a despotic society. In the

---

[174] Inter-American Commission on Human Rights in its Report on Cuba, http://www.fiu.edu/~fcf/IACHR.html
[175] CRC Committee, *Concluding Observations: Georgia* (UN Doc. CRC/C/15/Add.222, 2003), paras. 28–29.
[176] *Cf.* discussion on Harry Kalven's theory in J. Rawls, *Political Liberalism* (New York, Columbia University, 1996), p. 342.
[177] H. Kalven quoted in: A. Lewis, *Make No Law: The Sullivan Case and the First Amendment* (USA Vintage Books, 1992), p. 53.

words of Kalven, 'political freedom ends when government can use its powers and its courts to silence its critics'.[178]

97. The instrumental value of freedom of expression in ECHR jurisprudence is to begin with defined in terms of the paramount protection afforded to political speech.[179] The ECtHR attaches the highest importance to the freedom of expression in the context of political debate and considers that very strong reasons are required to justify restrictions on political speech.[180]

98. The Human Rights Committee issued a decision in March 2005 confirming the essential function of the freedom of political expression in democracy, finding that the Angolan government had breached a number of a journalist's fundamental rights.[181] The Committee held that the journalist's conviction and sentence following his criticism of the Angolan President constituted an unlawful interference with his right to freedom of expression: 'Given the paramount importance, in a democratic society, of the right to freedom of expression and of a free and uncensored press or other media, the severity of the sanctions imposed on the author cannot be considered as a proportionate measure to protect public order or the honour and the reputation of the President, a public figure who, as such, is subject to criticism and opposition. In addition, the Committee considers it an aggravating factor that the author's proposed truth defence against the libel charge was ruled out by the courts.'[182]

99. Article 13 of the ACHR is the only one of the above mentioned human rights instruments that actually affords protection against insidious restraints. The Inter-American Court of Human Rights had an opportunity to address fully the scope of the prohibition on prior censorship in Article 13 of the

---

[178] ECtHR, *Lingens* v. *Austria*, Judgment of 8 July 1986, *Publications of the Court*, Series A, 103; ECtHR, *Observer and Guardian* v. *the United Kingdom*, Judgment of 26 November 1991, *Publications of the Court*, Series A, 216.

[179] ECtHR, *Feldek* v. *Slovakia*, Judgment of 12 July 2001, *Reports* 2001–VIII, para. 83.

[180] UN Human Rights Committee CCPR/C/D/1128/2202, 29 March 2005. (Rafael Marques de Morais, an Angolan journalist, was arrested and imprisoned in Luanda, on October 16, 1999, following the publication in the Agora newspaper of remarks by him about Angolan President José Eduardo dos Santos. Among other things, Marques said that the President was responsible 'for the destruction of the country' and 'accountable for the promotion of incompetence, embezzlement and corruption.' Marques was detained for forty days without charges, ten of them incommunicado.)

[181] Human Rights Committee, *Rafael Marques v. Angola*, Decision of 29 March 2005, UN Doc. CCPR/C/D/1128/2202, para. 68.

[182] Inter-American Court of Human Rights, *Olmedo Bustos et al. v. Chile* Merits ('The Last Temptation of Christ' case), Series C No. 73, Judgment of 5 February 2001.

ACHR in the *Last Temptation of Christ case*.[183] The case involved the prohibition in Chile of the exhibition of the film and the IACtHR noted that Article 13 of the ACHR does not allow prior censorship, with the exception of prior censorship of public entertainments for the sole purpose of regulating access to them for the moral protection of childhood and adolescence. As the ban on the film applied to adults as well as to children and adolescents, it violated the Article 13 of the ACHR prohibition of prior censorship. The Court submitted that with regard to Article 13 of the ACHR, the State must modify its legal system because it is obliged to respect the right to freedom of expression and to guarantee its free and full exercise to all persons subject to its jurisdiction. It stated that in 'international law, customary law establishes that a State which has ratified a human rights treaty must introduce the necessary modifications to its domestic law to ensure the proper compliance with the obligations it has assumed. This law is universally accepted and is supported by jurisprudence. The ACHR establishes the general obligation of each State Party to adapt its domestic law to the provisions of the Convention, in order to guarantee the rights it embodies. This general obligation of the State Party implies that the measure of domestic law must be effective (the principle of *effet utile*). This means that the State must adopt all measures so that the provisions of the Convention are effectively fulfilled in its domestic legal system, as Article 2 of the Convention requires. Such measures are only effective when the State adjusts its actions to the Convention's rules on protection'.[184]

100. Article 4 of the CRC describes obligations of the States Parties, which are obligations of *conduct* rather than of *result*. Emphasis is put on general measures, including those of a political nature, to make reality of the principles and provisions of the CRC.[185] The objectives of the CRC to promote social progress and better standards of life in larger freedom[186] are not conceivable without active public support. Children who are raised in fear of public criticism are not likely to act upon their opinions when they grow up, which is not to the benefit of any society. Such atmosphere was described

[183] *Ibid.*, paras. 87–88.
[184] *Cf.* T. Hammarberg, *l.c.* (note 59), pp. 362–363.
[185] As stated in the CRC Preamble.
[186] Attorney Floyd Abrams, 10 Med. L. Rprt. para. 17, 24. 4. 1984, News Notes, quoted in D.L. Teeter, D.R. Le Duc and B. Loving, *Law of Mass Communications: Freedom and Control of Print and Broadcast Media,* Ninth Edition (USA, Foundation Press, 1998), p. 214.

by US Supreme Court Justice William Brennan in what has been termed 'the most far reaching, extraordinary and beautiful decisions in American history'[187] when he said that the 'pall of fear and timidity imposed upon those who would give voice to public criticism' is an atmosphere in which freedom of speech cannot survive.[188]

---

[187] *New York Times Co.* v. *Sullivan,* 376 US 254 (1964).
[188] As stated in the Preamble to the CRC.

CONCLUSION

RETHINKING INNOCENCE?

102. There are various obstacles in the way of the child's right to freedom of expression. The CRC Committee has pointed out the lack of legal guarantees for the freedom of expression for children below 18 years of age within the States Parties to the CRC. It has also expressed concern with regard to the inadequate attention given to the promotion of and respect for the right of the child to freedom of expression due to prevailing traditional, societal attitudes. Most States have apparently not yet adopted the meaning of this right in the 19th century sense of Mill, which is a right not to be coerced by anyone, government or groups in society. Secondly, it is a duty to form an opinion for the sake of the 'welfare of mankind', which is analogous to 'improving the living conditions of children in every country'.[189] Cultural obstacles pose a real threat whether they stem from religious dogma, oppressive political culture or corrupt business tactics in exploiting children with vulgarity and violence or simply apathy resulting from ignorance, lack of information and/or mindless consumerism.

103. The issue of the States' positive obligations in securing what ought to be *de lege ferenda* effective rights in accordance with obligations under human rights treaties has been dealt with by the ECtHR which accentuates that the scope of the States Parties' obligations inevitably vary depending on the diversity of the situations within these States, difficulties involved in implementation and not least, choices which must be made in terms of priorities and resources.[190] Positive obligations may not be interpreted in such a way as to impose an impossible or disproportionate burden on the authorities.[191] The CRC Committee has emphasized the State's obligation in ensuring children's access to information.[192] It has also emphasized the need for

---

[189] Cf. ECtHR, *Ösgur Gündem v. Turkey*, Judgement of 16 March 2000, *Reports* 2000–III. Cf. H. Thorgeirsdóttir, *o.c.* (note 26), p. 11.

[190] ECtHR, *Ösgur Gündem v. Turkey*, Judgement of 16 March 2000, *Reports* 2000–III para. 43, citing *Rees v. the United Kingdom*, 17 October 1986, Series A no. 106, para. 37; *Osman v. the United Kingdom* [GC], 28 October 1998, RJD 1998–VIII, para. 116.

[191] CRC Committee, *Concluding Observations: Kazakhstan* (UN Doc. CRC/C15/Add. 213, 2003).

[192] CRC Committee, *Day of General Discussion on the Child and the Media,* (UN Doc. CRC/C/57, 1996), paras. 242–257.

budgetary support to ensure the production and dissemination of literary and media material to children.[193] The CRC Committee in a recommendation on the private sector as service provider and its role in implementing child rights, emphasizes that ultimately the States Parties to the CRC have the primary responsibility for compliance with its provisions with regard to all persons within its jurisdiction. They have a legal obligation to respect and ensure the rights of children as stipulated in the Convention, which includes the obligation to ensure that non-State service providers operate in accordance with its provisions, thus creating indirect obligations on such actors. The State continues to be bound by its political obligations under the treaty, even when the provision of services is delegated to non-State actors.[194]

104. The 1924 Declaration of the Rights of the Child adopted the general principle that 'mankind owes to the child the best it has to give'. This could also be paraphrased in saying that the best the world can get derives from children. Rousseau, who in the 18th century taught parents to take a new interest in their children and to educate differently, emphasized the furtherance of expression of emotion rather than polite restraint and reached the conclusion that modern progress had corrupted instead of improved men. He believed that man is good by nature but had been corrupted by society and civilisation. The belief in man's natural goodness was the cornerstone of his argument. There are natural distinctions arising from differences in strength and intelligence. And there are artificial distinctions based on conventions that govern societies. He believed that inequality of men is one of the features of the long process by which men become alienated from nature and from innocence. Rousseau proposed that man would return to nature.

105. Children have for long been deprived of any direct representation of their own interests.[195] The CRC was to have a significant impact on the participation rights of children.[196] It was not however the intention of the drafters of the CRC to grant children an actual right to political participa-

---

[193] CRC Committee, *Recommendation: The Private Sector as Service Provider and its Role in Implementing Child Rights* (UN Doc. CRC/C/121, 2002).

[194] *Cf.* UN Doc. E/CN.4/Sub.2/1991/42.

[195] G. Van Bueren, *o.c.* (note 3), p. 131.

[196] *Travaux Préparatoires* (UN Doc.E/CN.4/1988/28, 1988), pp. 9–13. *Cf.* also S. Detrick, *o.c.* (note 16), para. 36, p. 233.

tion; an effective exercise of freedom of expression through voting.[197] Conferring such a right and corresponding responsibilities on children is commonly not considered wise as children are seen as immature and easy to exploit. The manipulation of public opinion is however not confined to children nor are they to blame for the abuse of power where adults participate in politics. No country in the world is immune from corruption in politics.[198] The roots of this vast corruption are complex but corporate financing over the political process is one of the main reasons.[199] There is not much that children can do in the face of such immense power of finance and politics, interfering with the public's ability to exercise their civil and political rights in most States of the world. The UN Human Development Report 2004[200] encourages allowing people full expression, including the poor and the marginalized and not least youth, to prevent outbursts of violence. The UN Report praises legal protection and guarantees for minorities and other groups as a critical foundation for broader freedoms yet stating that unless the political culture changes, real changes will not happen.[201]

106. Some say that denying children suffrage constitutes political discrimination and exclusion.[202] The CRC Committee is particularly concerned about *de facto* discrimination, including multiform-discrimination against vulnerable groups of children[203] – perhaps without sufficiently linking the horrendous situation of hundreds of millions of children to their actual lack of exercising their civil and political rights. Some serious rethinking and affirmative action in this area might lead to substantial reforms. Perhaps it is time to turn to the innocent.

---

[197] *Cf. Transparency International Global Corruption Report 2005*. The *Global Corruption Report 2005* is published in London by Pluto Press. It is edited in Berlin by Diana Rodriguez, Gerard Waite and Toby Wolfe. Length: p. 316. Essays examine the role of money in politics assessing the regulation of political party financing, suggesting ways to rewire the arms and oil trades for greater transparency and analysing the problem of vote buying. Reports consider attempts to repatriate assets stolen by politicians, disclosure regulations, the nexus between the media, politics and business as well as the issue of immunity from prosecution with special insight into extradition efforts in the Fujimori case in Peru.

[198] *Ibid.*

[199] United Nations Human Development Reoprt 2004, *Cultural Liberty in Today's Diverse World?* (New York, UNDP, 2004).

[200] *Ibid.*, foreword by Mark Malloch Brown, Administrator UNDP.

[201] B. Franklin (ed.), *The Rights of Children* (Oxford, Basil Blackwell, 1986), p. 24.

[202] CRC Committee, *Concluding Oberservations: Philippines* (UN Doc. CRC/C/15/Add.258, 2005).

[203] B. Franklin (ed.), *o.c.* (note 201), p. 24.